on track ...

The
Doors

every album, every song

Tony Thompson

SONICBOND

sonicbondpublishing.com

Sonicbond Publishing Limited
www.sonicbondpublishing.co.uk
Email: info@sonicbondpublishing.co.uk

First Published in the United Kingdom 2021
First Published in the United States 2021

British Library Cataloguing in Publication Data:
A Catalogue record for this book is available from the British Library

ISBN 978-1-78952-137-

Typeset in ITC Garamond & ITC Avant Garde
Printed and bound in England

Graphic design and typesetting: Full Moon Media

on track ...
The Doors

Contents

Introduction – Band from Venice

It's the spring of 1966, a warm evening in West Hollywood. You and a couple of friends are heading down the Sunset strip looking for a small club called London Fog. Someone said that there was a good band playing there. The singer is supposed to be an acid poet or something, a total freak, and the other guys can really play. They are like The Seeds but better, apparently.

It's a tiny place with a small stage at the back. There is a dancer in a cage on one side and the band squeezed into the other. The first thing that you notice is the drummer. There is no bass player, so this guy is holding the whole thing down. The keyboard player is firing off little riffs on a Vox organ but is also covering the bass parts on a Fender Rhodes. The guitarist is on a journey with flamenco flourishes and bent blue notes. The singer is screaming something about fire.

Over at the bar, the owner of London Fog is shaking his head. The dancer in the cage looks alarmed and self-conscious. Everyone is watching the singer. He looks like a surfer, a sort of all-American tripper who might have been the quarterback on his high school football team before he tried LSD. Then again, he might have been the loner reading *Beyond Good and Evil* in the library at lunchtime. Now he is the lead singer in a band that supposedly had a contract with Columbia but was dropped before they recorded anything. The bar is half full of prostitutes, out of work actors, runaways, scene makers, junkies, students, and barflies. You look around and think, these people have found their band.

This is the Beginning

The ur-Doors were a frat rock outfit called Rick & The Ravens. The band included two brothers, originally from Chicago, who had moved to Redondo Beach. They were Rick and Jim Manzcarek (Ray later dropped the c from his surname) on organ and guitar. They were often joined by their older brother, who called himself Screaming Ray Daniels when he played the piano and sang with them. He was a graduate film student at UCLA who already had a degree in economics. The band played frat houses, student pubs, bar mitzvahs, and beach parties. Their set was designed to get people dancing and they covered anything with a beat.

Rick & The Ravens recorded three singles which, if not for the fact that the band morphed into one of the most popular rock and roll acts of all time, would be fodder for the folks who compile compilation albums of West Coast garage music. The singles aren't terrible, just not terribly promising. They were all recorded in the first half of 1965.

'Soul Train'/ 'Geraldine' (Aura Records 4511)

Soul Train is a rewrite of Gary US Bonds' 1960 single, 'New Orleans'. Ray does pretty well as a growling lead singer and if you could squint with your ears, you might be able to find a scrap of his more familiar organ work in The Doors. It's a pretty good approximation of Gary US Bonds' frat rock style but not remarkable or unique in any sense. 'Geraldine' is more of the same. You can imagine jugs of beer and a lot of slightly sozzled students on the dancefloor. The single is nicely arranged and, by the standards of the time, well-produced.

'Henrietta'/ 'Just For You' (Aura Records 4506)

The party continues with Henrietta. Ray's singing is better on this one and it might be the pick of the bunch. It's a Lucille-style shouter that doesn't turn any new ground but has enough fire to keep you listening. The flip side is similar fare.

'Big Bucket T'/ 'Rampage' (Posae Records 101)

Big Bucket T is driven by a honking sax and Ray's blues piano lines. The car in question is described in detail and there are some automotive sound effects. Again, nothing wrong with it but Rick & The Ravens weren't going to wrestle pop music back from the UK invaders in 1965. The B-side, 'Rampage' is an agreeable instrumental with crowd noises to give it a live sound.

Rick & The Ravens' main gig was a bar on Santa Monica Blvd called the Turkey Joint West, where the crowd was mostly made up of Ray's film school buddies. One night, a drunken student kept hollering out for 'Louie Louie'. The band was starting to find it annoying, but Ray knew the drunk and invited him up to sing the song. Jim Morrison made his rock and roll debut that night.

Later, in the summer of 1965, after they had both graduated from UCLA, Ray and Jim happened to run into each other on Venice Beach. This meeting is one of the most famous stories in rock and roll. Ray Manzarek is probably responsible for the more mythic proportions of the tale as it stands, but it remains one of those moments like Keith and Mick on the train or John and Paul at the church fete. The two recent graduates knew each other quite well by this point, but Ray thought Jim had moved to New York and was surprised to see his friend wandering, shirtless and starry-eyed, down the beach. The younger man had lost weight and was living on the roof of a nearby apartment building (now the Morrison Apartments at 14 Westminster Ave, Venice, CA). He was also writing songs. Cajoled by Ray into singing one of them, he came out with 'Moonlight Drive'. Now go back and listen to 'Geraldine' by Rick & The Ravens. Yes, Ray was astonished. Nowadays, Ray or Jim would have recorded the entire episode on an iPhone and put it on Instagram, but we will have to use our imaginations to recapture how the song sounded that day.

Rick & The Ravens were out of contract with a small label called Aura Records, but Ray convinced Rick Bock, the owner of World Pacific Records (which owned Aura), to let them make a demo tape of Jim's songs. With his brothers, a bass player named Patty Sullivan, and his new Transcendental Meditation friend John Densmore on drums, he and Jim committed to tape a group of songs, all of which sound a million miles away from the party rock of Rick & The Ravens. The session took place in September of 1965 at the legendary World Pacific Studios in a neighbourhood called Beverly Grove near West Hollywood. If you want to make a pilgrimage, the studio is now called Arch Angel and is owned by Neil Diamond. Rick & The Ravens recorded six songs that day: 'Moonlight Drive', 'Hello, I Love You', 'Summer's Almost Gone', 'My Eyes Have Seen You, 'End Of The Night' and 'Go Insane'.

These are important recordings in The Doors story. You can hear them, along with the Rick & The Ravens singles, on YouTube, but they are all available on The Doors 1997 *Box Set* collection. Most bands have a fuller pre-flight catalogue. Led Zeppelin fans, for example, can pick through The Yardbirds' *Little Games* or Robert Plant's various pre-Zep efforts. A group like The Band might seem to have arrived out of nowhere in 1968 but had been making recordings both as a backing band and as Levon And The Hawks for almost ten years when that first album appeared. These six songs are it for The Doors, along with a live recording that I will get to soon.

Something of Rick & The Ravens remains in this version of 'Hello I Love You'. Anyone who believes the chord progression was a rip off of The Kinks' 'All Day and All of the Night' should listen to this demo. Ray is drawing on the same '50s RnB ideas that underpinned much of the frat rock of the period. The Kinks were probably drawing on a similar source. 'Moonlight Drive' gets the RnB treatment as well. With Ray's brother Jim on harmonica where Robby's slide guitar will one day appear, it could be an Excello Records B-side, except, of course, for the lyrics.

'End Of The Night' is creepy and surprisingly similar in arrangement to the version that would appear on the band's first album eighteen months later. It's more garage than frat and Jim finds his real voice on the second 'realms of bliss...' section where he begins to belt the lyrics. He sounds like he is experimenting with a more Dylanesque delivery up until then. Keeping in mind that he had, save for one drunken version of 'Louie Louie', never sung on stage or been in a band, he does exceptionally well on 'End Of The Night' to deliver the lyrics so convincingly.

This version of 'Summer's Almost Gone' almost beats the later album version for atmosphere and groove. It's missing Robby's slide guitar, but Jim's voice is less mannered and the emotion of the song is perhaps more obvious. As will be noted, I think this song is underrated but, of all of these demos, this is the one that I go back to most often. The better-known version is majestic and dark but loses some of the whimsy heard here.

The other two songs on the demo are 'My Eyes Have Seen You' and 'Go Insane'. If The Doors had stopped after this session, I suspect that both of these would have been highly sought after garage punk recordings. 'Go Insane' which reappears in the 'Celebration Of The Lizard' suite, is verging on novelty in the tradition of 'They're Coming To Take Me Away'. 'My Eyes Have Seen You' is a blueprint for the later versions but with the harmonica in the mix and the pounding piano chords, it is well into Nuggets territory.

I'm always surprised when these demos are dismissed as juvenilia or as unrepresentative of The Doors' later work. What is surprising, particularly with Rick & The Ravens' three singles in mind, is how far along The Doors were at this stage. Robby was not yet in the picture and this is only two months after the famous beach meeting. It's amazing that they resemble the band at all. Only one of these songs, 'End Of The Night', appeared on their first album. The others, except for 'Go Insane', all turned up on *Strange Days*. If you are curious about the development of the band's sound, this is the place to start.

So, what happened between the beach and the studio? There is no question that Jim's lyrics had a profound effect on Ray. They seemed to have provided permission to stretch out musically. The summer of 1965 saw the release of Bob Dylan's *Highway 61 Revisited* album. With 'Like A Rolling Stone' on the radio, it's easy to imagine Ray and Jim thinking that more sophisticated lyrics required a richer musical setting. Ray Manzarek doesn't mention the 1965 Watts Riots in his memoir, but the darkness in Jim's lyrics and the minor chords creeping into Ray's arrangements almost seem to evoke a different LA from the hopeful sounds of early sixties California bands like The Beach Boys.

The demo did not grab any of the record company people that they played it for in the fall of 1965. Unlike, say, a group of kids in Nebraska, The Doors were able to get around to record companies in person. Not that it did them any good. Lou Adler, who was finding great success with Jim's old high school classmate, Ellen Cohen, now known as Mama Cass, listened to the recordings and said that he couldn't use them. 'We don't want to be used anyway,' said Jim

Morrison. I'm sure they were all disappointed by Adler's lack of interest, but it's not easy to imagine The Doors on a label with The Mamas and Papas, Barry McGuire and The Grass Roots. Listen to the latter band's 'Let's Live For Today' if you want some sense of how The Doors might have sounded on Dunhill Records. It was never going to work.

But at least Adler was polite. Another executive at a different record company listened to a couple of seconds of 'Go Insane' before chasing them out of his office, screaming, 'get out of here, you potheads!' Incredibly, Columbia Records signed them in late 1965. The line-up of Jim, Ray, Robby and John was established by this point, but the band was still playing the sort of gigs that Rick & The Ravens had done. Fortunately, Billy James, a hip young executive at Columbia, caught a whiff of something in those demos and signed them up.

But Columbia, surely to their regret, did nothing with the band. After giving them an advance and some free equipment, including a Vox Organ for Ray, they simply ignored them. Around this time, after auditioning for a bass player, Ray got hold of a Fender Rhodes piano bass and solved the problem. Somehow, the bass guitar never sounded right to the band. John Densmore told Mick Wall that Patty Sullivan, who played on the demos, made them sound like the Stones. Apparently, that was a bad thing! They auditioned others but came away thinking that the Fender Rhodes was the better option.

Sometime in early 1966, The Doors were able to secure a residency at London Fog, a small bar in West Hollywood. The crowds were pretty thin and despite some accounts to the contrary, this is not where The Doors first found their wider audience. What they found was their sound and onstage identity. Jim started the residency almost too shy to face the crowd and ended it as the provocative performance poet whose style continues to influence lead singers. London Fog was The Doors' Hamburg. It was here that the seeds that can be heard on the 1965 demo flowered. Malcolm Gladwell uses The Beatles period in Germany to illustrate his 10,000 hours theory of mastery. Night after night, The Doors were able to experiment with their sound and refine it in front of small crowds.

Fortunately, there is a live recording from that period, and in December of 2016, it was released by Rhino Records as *London Fog 1966*. The recordings were made by a UCLA student called Netti Pena, and along with the demos, are pretty much all there is on tape of The Doors until the first album. No recordings have surfaced of the famous shows at Whisky A Go Go where they spent the summer of 1966, or at the Ondine Theatre in New York, where they played a month's worth of gigs later in the year. The next live recordings available date from early 1967, almost a year later – a long gap in 1960s rock and roll time!

London Fog 1966

Recorded: May 1966 at the London Fog, West Hollywood CA
Released: December 2016
Label: Rhino/Bright Midnight Archives
Producer: Bruce Botnick
Chart: N/A
Running Time: 32:04

For reasons that aren't entirely clear, the recordings made available here do not represent the entire set that they were playing at the time. When they appeared in 2016, Robby Kreiger implied that he had heard the full tape and that it included 'Light My Fire'. John Densmore has said that they were doing originals along with the covers that make up most of the album. It is interesting, however, to consider how important Chicago style blues was to their early sound when it also shaped the later stages of the band's direction before Morrison's death.

'Tuning'
Always a good idea.

'Rock Me' (Waters)
'Rock Me' is a blues standard with deep roots and an extensive legacy. Lil Son Jackson's 'Rockin And Rollin' (1951) is generally viewed as the source for better-known versions by Muddy Waters and BB King, but that song was itself based on 'Rockin' Chair' by Big Bill Broonzy or perhaps Arthur Crudup's 'Rock Me Mama'. Jackson's version was the basis for Slim Harpo's best-known song, 'I'm A King Bee'. Old Crow Medicine Show's more recent hit 'Rock Me Mama' is based on a Dylan fragment which itself is almost certainly based on the standard. Led Zeppelin's version of Muddy Water's 'You Shook Me' is part of the family too.

The Doors deliver it up here in a slow and mildly lascivious manner. BB King's recording was the more recent, but I suspect that Ray, the boy from Chicago, based this on Muddy's rendition. Robby seems to be faintly echoing Bob Dylan's most recent single at the time, 'Rainy Day Women 12 & 35' at points, although it is a standard blues guitar line that he is playing. As the song builds, it is clear that Jim is finding his voice. His explosive style that becomes something of a signature appears in the final verse. They revisited this one during the *Morrison Hotel* sessions, but it wasn't included on the album. 'Cars Hiss By My Window', at the other end of their short career, employs the same arrangement.

'Baby Please Don't Go' (Williams)
This is another blues standard with deep roots. The first version under this title was by Big Joe Williams in 1935, but it was covered by John Lee Hooker,

Muddy Waters, and many others in subsequent years. Ray Manzarek was no doubt aware of Muddy's recording, but the likely source here is the 1959 single by Hooker. It's interesting to note that it does not seem to be based on the terrifying version by Them, the Belfast band fronted by Van Morrison. Robby's guitar work is decidedly Hooker-esque and does not employ the famous Them riff. In any case, Morrison finishes the song hollering the title in the same manner that he will one day do with the phrase 'city at night'.

'You Make Me Real' (The Doors)
The first real Doors song on the album sounds, interestingly, like a throwback to Rick & The Ravens, albeit with a much rowdier sound. This is glorious mid-sixties garage punk with a growling Morrison leading the charge and Robby submitting a suitably surf-style guitar break. This song appears on *Morrison Hotel* later in the story and will be discussed further but prepare to fall in love with this version if you haven't heard it.

'Tuning'
Still a good idea.

'Don't Fight It' (Cropper, Pickett)
This doesn't come off nearly as well as the preceding blues covers, but it is an interesting choice. It was written by Wilson Pickett and Steve Cropper and was a hit for the former in 1965. The Doors' version is pure garage and fairly loose. The original is not as well remembered as other hits by Pickett, but it is one of his best. The point might be that Morrison was exploring the vocal styles of singers like Pickett as he developed his own voice. Pickett is one of the most convincing vocalists of the era and on song after song, he sounded like he thought he might never get another chance to tell his story. Jim was listening.

'I'm Your Hootchie Cootchie Man' (Dixon)
This is another blues standard though it is mainly associated with Muddy Waters and the song's composer, Willie Dixon. Ray takes the lead vocal here while Jim wails on harmonica. His harp work is enthusiastic, just not very good. You can hear The Doors' blues sound coming together here. Robby's fills are probably the most familiar element. It's a bit chaotic, but the crowd seems to enjoy it.

'Strange Days' (The Doors)
This is likely the song of most interest to fans. Hopefully, at some point, more recordings will appear of other early versions of Doors classics. 'Strange Days' is an eerie song anyway, but hearing it in such a raw form underscores the atmosphere conveyed in the lyrics. It later appeared on their second album of the same name and is one of their best-known cuts. Here, in the context

of the raw blues covers, it points the way forward. It's a primitive version but is essentially all there. Without the whole set, it is impossible to know how it would have fit in, but everything from the chord changes to the lyrics set this song apart from the other material on *London Fog*. I will look into this song in more detail in the *Strange Days* album section.

'Lucille' (Collins, Richard)
Surely a holdover from the Rick & The Ravens days, this Little Richard song is done in a fairly plodding manner. That said, Jim is in good voice here and it is interesting to hear what he does with the lyrics.

Jim Morrison's Library: The Bookworm King

The name of the band comes from William Blake's *The Marriage Of Heaven And Hell*. 'If the doors of perception were cleansed, everything would appear to man as it is, Infinite.' It was in the same volume that Blake also suggested that 'the road of excess leads to the palace of wisdom', a sentiment that Morrison surely found to his liking. The name of the band was probably partially inspired by Aldous Huxley's 1954 book, *The Doors Of Perception,* which outlined his experiences with mescaline.

Jim Morrison was, according to his friends and family, an avid reader with wide interests. His lyrics are not overwhelmed with literary allusions, but they are certainly there and provide something of a glimpse at his bookshelf. Like many young people of his generation and those that followed, he read Jack Kerouac's *On The Road* and was deeply influenced by it. The actor Johnny Depp once wrote an essay for *Rolling Stone* called 'Kerouac, Ginsberg, The Beats And Other Bastards Who Ruined My Life'. It's a pretty accurate description of the effect that a deep dive into the Beats can have on one's teenage years. The 1956 novel told the story of a series of road trips undertaken by the narrator, Sal Paradise, and his friend Dean Moriarty. Essentially, it is about freedom and the joy of living life on one's own terms. The book was enormously influential on the counterculture of the 1960s. As Bob Dylan said, 'I read *On The Road* in maybe 1959. It changed my life like it changed everyone else's.' Kerouac was a highly spiritual writer, a cradle Catholic, who was fascinated by Buddhism. In addition to using the road as a metaphor, Jim Morrison also absorbed Kerouac's metaphysical exuberance into his work.

Nobody just reads *On The Road*. It is a gateway drug that will soon lead the reader to Allen Ginsberg's 'Howl', Gregory Corso's 'Gasoline', William Burrough's novel, *Naked Lunch* and a lot of other works by writers gathered under the Beat and/or San Francisco Renaissance label. All of them were fearless with language and employed metaphor lavishly. Ginsberg and Corso were themselves inspired by the Romantics, including (if you count him as one) William Blake. It's not hard to spot the Beat influence in something like 'Horse Latitudes'.

Jim Morrison's philosophical ideas around revolution, unlike many of his Marxist contemporaries, seemed to be inspired by Friedrich Nietzsche, whose ideas included the 'death of God' and the rise of the 'superman'. His passionate writing sought to describe a new way of living that broke free of society's morals and expectations. Jim Morrison, not surprisingly, found his philosophy enormously interesting.

An entire book has been devoted to similarities between Jim Morrison and the French nineteenth-century symbolist poet Arthur Rimbaud. Patti Smith has regularly made the connection between the two as well. Rimbaud's most famous work, 'A Season In Hell', is a long-form poem that one can imagine appealing to Jim Morrison.

John Rechy's 1963 novel *City Of Night* which depicted the seedy underworld of Los Angeles, appears to have been a great favourite of Jim Morrison, judging from his use of the title in the song 'L.A. Woman'. Colleagues of Jim have also mentioned Norman Mailer's *The Deer Park* as a book he often recommended to people. The now almost forgotten novel is set in Hollywood and goes to great lengths to highlight the sleaziness of the movie industry. Joan Didion called The Doors the 'Norman Mailers of Rock and Roll', which no doubt would have appealed to Morrison, though perhaps not to Mailer.

Much has been written about Jim Morrison's literary influences. Throughout his work, there are the sort of echoes and resonances that one might expect from someone who had spent his young life reading. Critics have spotted a wide range of references in his work. Whether these are deliberate, unconscious, or accidental is impossible to know. I have tried, where possible and relevant, to identify these in my descriptions of his songs.

Hollywood Garage: The Sound of The Doors

There is a tendency to regard The Doors as a genre unto themselves in rock and roll. They were a remarkably original band in many ways, and it is hard to think of any band of that era who sounded like them. John Densmore believes that the lack of a permanent bass player meant that the other instruments occupied a slightly different space than they might have in a more traditional line-up. His own drumming, he felt, was about working with the other instruments rather than just pounding out a backbeat. Robby's guitar playing developed throughout The Doors career. His rhythm work is lyrical and influenced by his interest in flamenco and acoustic blues. His lead playing is tasteful and clever. Similarly, Ray's organ playing is never overwrought or intrusive. None of them had extensive experience as rock and roll performers and, in a sense, learned on the job as members of an ensemble. They grew as musicians, listening to each other. It's clear on some live recordings that Jim is not at his best, but the band was never anything but incredibly tight. Jerry Garcia, who was not a fan of Jim or the band in general, said they were stiff and that The Dead blew them off the stage every time they played together. Yeah right! In some ways, the two bands were reflections of each other in their respective cities. Both incorporated long jams and improvised sequences into their live shows. I don't want to start a war, but I know whose live recordings I prefer, and they don't include anything called St Stephen!

And there was Jim's voice. The whole question of who is a 'good singer' in rock and roll is vexed. Most people can agree that Jimi Hendrix was an extraordinary guitar player but ask who is a good singer and watch the sparks fly. I think Jim Morrison is one of the great vocalists. He was essentially a baritone, but his range stretched up to tenor territory. His heroes were Sinatra and Presley and his phrasing owed more to them than the growling blues singers whose work he covered. One of the striking things about Morrison's singing is his timing. For an untrained singer, he understood where he fit into an arrangement. Even when he was supposedly drunk and barely able to stand, as was the case with the studio recording of 'Five To One' apparently, he never missed. There is studio footage where he appears to be inebriated, but when the band begins, he comes in at precisely the right time. It's hard to overstate the importance of Jim's voice to The Doors' overall sound. There were a lot of great bands around in 1967. Very few of them had a vocalist as skilled and distinctive as Jim Morrison.

Their originality sometimes makes them seem like they appeared out of the ether, but like any band, they were subject to the chronological forces that placed them in the mid-sixties and the geographical forces that set their story in LA. 1966, when the band was finding their sound, was what might be termed the year of 'peak garage'. While the band themselves were fans of Chicago blues (Ray), Flamenco (Robby), Hard Bop (John) and early rock and roll (Jim), they were playing on bills with the bands of their own time. At the Whisky, they opened for, among others, Paul Butterfield Blues Band, The

Rascals, The Turtles, The Seeds, Love, Frank Zappa, Them, The Animals, The Beau Brummels, Buffalo Springfield, and Captain Beefheart. Alan Price's organ sound, Mike Bloomfield's guitar work, Van Morrison's rumbling menace, Love's romantic beauty, Zappa's audacity, Beefheart's blues madness, and the serious cool of The Seeds are all discernible in the early work of The Doors. If they hadn't scored such major hits and become a mainstay of 'classic rock', they might have instead been remembered as one of the great Hollywood garage bands.

But the garage element is complemented by other strands of music that were emerging in the mid-sixties. According to John Densmore, they were all fans of the landmark *Getz/Gilberto* album and Antonio Carlos Jobim's subsequent work. On the first album in particular, bossa nova is part of the sound. Like every other band, they were keenly aware of The Beatles' studio masterpieces, and an album like *The Soft Parade* was, to some extent, an attempt to move beyond the sound of their live sets. The last two albums reveal the influence of both blues rock and the back to basics ethic that prevailed as the decade ended. In a few tantalising moments on those albums, there are even glimpses of what Jim might have done as a 'singer-songwriter' in the decade that followed. *Full Circle*, the final album, and their second without Morrison, reveals, at points, their capacity for jazz rock. They are a unique band, but putting them in the context of what was a rich and varied period in rock and roll makes them all the more interesting.

The Movie Will Begin in Five Minutes: Cinema and The Doors

Eve Babitz once said of Jim Morrison that he was 'pure Hollywood'. Barney Hoskyns noted that The Doors represented the 'noir version of the California surfing dream'. Ray Manzarek said that Jim Morrison's whole Lizard King look was based on Marlon Brando's character in the 1960 Sidney Lumet film, *The Fugitive Kind*. It's almost impossible to imagine The Doors coming from any other place than Los Angeles. Keeping in mind that two members of the band had degrees in film studies, it isn't difficult to identify the cinematic qualities in Morrison's stories and the band's dramatic music. Think of 'The End'.

'The killer awoke before dawn, he put his boots on.' It reads like a script as Morrison directs the scene to its shocking finish. Is it any surprise that Francis Ford Coppola was able to use that song so effectively in *Apocalypse Now*? 'Roadhouse Blues' is pure film noir. You can picture Tom Neal and Ann Savage driving through the night in *Detour* (1945) or Robert Mitchum and Virginia Huston travelling through the desert in *Out Of The Past* (1947) in those opening lines.

Morrison, despite his literary interests, had a cinematic imagination. The songs are rarely interior monologues. He sets the scene, describes the characters and uses a variety of shots to capture the essence of both. A song like 'Soul Kitchen' is filled with the sort of details that a director might include to build the scene of a late-night diner. 'People Are Strange' uses a camera angle detail like 'uneven streets' to underscore the singer's sense of alienation. 'L.A. Woman' sets the scene for a crime feature with 'Drivin' down your freeways / Midnight alleys roam / Cops in cars, the topless bars'. Jim Morrison would make an actual film called *HWY* in 1969, but his best cinematic work may be in his lyrics.

The Doors (1967)

Recorded: August – September 1966 at Sunset Sound Recorders, Hollywood, California
Released: January 1967
Label: Elektra
Producer: Paul Rothchild
Engineer: Bruce Botnick
Additional musicians: Larry Knetchel (bass guitar)
Running Time: 44:48
Highest Chart Position: US: 2 UK: Did not chart

This album has aged well. It made my heart race when I first heard it as a teenager in 1980. A few months ago, I watched my teenage son's face light up as he listened to it for the first time. I can't begin to imagine what it sounded like in 1967. It is a thrilling record and one of the great debuts in rock and roll history. None of The Doors had spent much time in a studio and none of them had ever played in a truly professional band. Jim Morrison had been singing for just over a year. Put on side one and let that sink in.

It was recorded at Sunset Sound Recorders, a popular studio in Hollywood. The producer was the Elektra house man, Paul Rothchild, who had recorded The Paul Butterfield Band's first two albums. Rothchild was not particularly interested in producing The Doors but did so as a favour to Elektra's boss, Jac Holzman, who had employed him after a drug bust in the early '60s. His involvement with Love's *Da Capo* album probably made him a natural choice anyway. He would go on to produce all of their records with Jim Morrison, except *L.A. Woman*. His relationship with Jim and his ability to get the best from the often difficult and/ or drunk singer is a key part of The Doors story and one sometimes underplayed by biographers. I have mixed feelings about his later work with The Doors, but there is no question that he knew exactly what to do with Jim's voice.

It was recorded in about a month on a basic four-track recorder. Jim was on one track, Ray and Robby on another, John on the third, and a fourth for overdubs and bass guitar. Larry Knetchel, a Wrecking Crew bass gun, is on most of the songs, as Rothchild felt that Ray's bass organ didn't have the necessary punch for a recording. Like many Wrecking Crew musicians, his credits are far too many to mention, but he did play the memorable piano part on Simon and Garfunkel's 'Bridge Over Troubled Water'.

Why is it such a great album? It's a tricky question, but it is true that this material, unlike that on some of their later records, had been polished, set after set, night after night in London Fog and later, Whisky A Go Go. This was the band at their hungriest. The competition was fierce as they played alongside musicians who would define the late '60s and, in some cases, the next 20 years of popular music. The garage band element of The Doors, a holdover from the Rick & The Ravens era, is still discernible here, but they are also responding to the challenge of Bob Dylan's *Highway 61 Revisited*, The Beatles *Rubber Soul*,

The Beach Boys' *Pet Sounds*, Frank Zappa's *Freak Out*, and their label mates, Love's astonishing *Forever Changes*. This album appears just as the album format is coming into its own as a rock and roll artform. Yes, there are songs designed to be hit singles, but there is also a sense that the album itself has to make a statement too. A song like 'The End' is a reasonably early example of a classic album track in the tradition of what Bob Dylan had already done with songs like 'It's All Over Now Baby Blue' and 'Desolation Row'.

The album was mixed in the fall of 1966 while The Doors played a month-long residency in New York at Ondines on East 59th Street and hung out with Andy Warhol's Factory crowd. It was released in January of 1967, and a month later, The Doors were playing their first tentative shows at The Fillmore in San Francisco, the staging ground for the massive cultural shift taking place in America, and indeed the world. Within six months, Jim Morrison would be a key counterculture icon.

Side One
'Break On Through (To The Other Side)' (Morrison, Manzarek, Kreiger, Densmore)

It's hard to think of a more exhilarating opening song on a debut album. Is it a drug song? A philosophical call to arms? A dark love song? A declaration of war on conformity? The beginning of Morrison's erotic revolution? It might be all of those and more.

It begins, as has been noted many times, in a similar manner to Them's 'One Two Brown Eyes'. John Densmore sets the tone with a stick and brush bossa nova beat before he is joined by Ray's bass organ essaying Ray Charles 'What I Say' and Robby's variation on the Paul Butterfield Band's Shake Your Money Maker. It's sampling, garage punk style, and there is astonishing tension in those few bars before Morrison begins to sing.

Night, as we will see, played a significant role in Jim's imagination. Day might destroy the night, but night still divides each day. After this verse, the song sounds vaguely like an elegy for a lost love. Several of these early songs were supposedly written for a high school girlfriend who had followed Jim to LA. Not surprisingly, the relationship did not survive Jim's conversion to LSD over the summer of 1965 when many of these songs were written.

But the exhortation to break on through to the other side is the most memorable aspect of the song. There is some idea that Jim thought this up while wandering around the canal area of the Venice neighbourhood of Los Angeles. There are numerous bridges, and perhaps something of the imagery of repeatedly crossing to the other side of the various canals appealed to him. It has been popularly regarded as a song about acid, but it could refer to any flavour of intellectual, spiritual or emotional breakthrough. Jim reportedly had little interest in eastern religions, but the implicit mysticism is present in any number of traditions. It's worth noting that the old spiritual about the 'deep and wide' Jordan River makes a brief appearance.

But the lyrics work because the arrangement suits them so well. The urgency of the main riff and the insistence of Densmore's drumming perfectly underscore the act or idea of breaking through. The organ solo is simple but effective. 'Latin' is Ray's comment on it in the Classic Albums episode about this album. It's followed by Jim's seemingly improvised line 'Everybody Loves My Baby', surely a reference to the Fats Waller song. Which version he was thinking of is anyone's guess, but it was something of a jug band standard in the mid-sixties. This is followed or would have been followed, by Jim shouting 'She gets high!', except that Elektra got cold feet here. Songs with the word 'high' in them were, in the mid-sixties, becoming an issue. The Byrds' 'Eight Miles High', written by white knuckle flyer Gene Clark, was widely believed to be a drug song and promptly banned by radio stations. Jim's lyrics didn't leave much room for interpretation, so the engineer, Bruce Botnick, simply edited them out. 'She gets uh… she gets uh….' It was more than thirty years before the restored version appeared.

It was the first song that was used on the album to be recorded, and it was completed in one session over a few hours. Elektra released it as a single, which remarkably failed to find its way into the *Billboard* Top 100. It was played at most of their shows and remains one of their best-known songs. It's not easy to understand why it wasn't a hit, but perhaps it works best as the opening salvo on the record. It's brief and seems like almost an overture to the songs to come.

It has been covered by a variety of acts, but never in a way that has even come close to topping the original or adding much to it. That said, Tom Wait's guitar player Marc Ribot's version is worth hearing. Fans of *The Simpsons* may recall Krusty The Clown showing a clip of himself singing it in 1973 and falling to the stage, Morrison style, howling 'yeahhhh'.

'Soul Kitchen' (Morrison, Manzarek, Kreiger, Densmore)

In the early 1980s, Ray Manzarek produced the first record by the Los Angeles band, X. X was part of the early punk scene in the city and Manzarek must have seemed like a slightly odd choice in the Year Zero atmosphere of the time. The Doors were undergoing their first of many revivals in the early '80s but were still something of a 'dinosaur' band. If you were a teenager at the time, you would recall that the lines between punk and hippie were pretty clear. But this turned out to be a wonderful matchup. Manzarek had been impressed with their lyrics and perhaps noted the LA noir themes as not being too far from some of Morrison's. The album is called *Los Angeles,* and among its many pleasures is a frantic cover of 'Soul Kitchen'. Somewhere on YouTube, there is a great clip of Manzarek singing it with X onstage. It's a bit hard to hear him, but there is something magic about his presence.

The Doors' original version is a slower and slyly funkier affair. Robby Kreiger has suggested that he was thinking of James Brown – perhaps the Godfather of Soul's timeless 'I Feel Good' when he created the nifty guitar riff that runs through the verses. It's a simple song musically that speaks to the more garage side of their sound. Greil Marcus suggests that it is a close relative of Them's 'Gloria', a song they covered on stage and certainly knew well.

The lyrics are a wonderful stream of consciousness set in the night world of the painter Edward Hopper or The Beat writers. The singer sits in a restaurant late at night, watching cars pass outside and wishing he could stay. The soul kitchen is a metaphor for warmth and belonging. The singer pleads that if he has to leave, he will wander and stumble in the 'neon groves'. The world outside is cold and unfriendly. He mentions cars 'full of eyes' in the first verse. There is something slightly lysergic about the paranoia in that line and phrases like 'warm my mind' are equally suggestive. There is fine detail, as well. 'Well, your fingers weave quick minarets / Speak in secret alphabets / I light another cigarette' is an evocative set of images. The repetition of 'learn to forget' is intriguing and sounds slightly mystical in this context.

This is one of Jim's early songs, written in the summer of 1965. The consensus is that the 'soul kitchen' in question was a restaurant called Olivia's Place in Venice that closed soon after but was located at the corner of Ocean Park and Main. It was cheap and a favourite of Jim's. As with 'Break On Through', the song was inspired by an actual place in Jim's noir version of Los Angeles.

It's a great song, and if they weren't going to release 'Light My Fire' as the first single, I think this would have been a better choice than 'Break On Through'. It doesn't have the call to arms punch, but the lyrics are more interesting, and Jim's phrasing is perfect for the story. It is among the second line of well-known Doors songs, after the hits. Along with X's version, the song has been covered occasionally over the years. Massive Doors fan Patti Smith's version on her covers album, *Twelve*, is an interesting interpretation. She slows it down slightly and brings the lyrics to the forefront. A version by Gomez, recorded for the *Jools Holland Show*, is worth watching on YouTube.

'The Crystal Ship' (Morrison, Manzarek, Kreiger, Densmore)

There is a tendency to turn all songs from the sixties into narcotic nod-nod wink-winks. John Lennon was reportedly stunned by the suggestion that Lucy in the Sky with Diamonds was code for LSD and various Byrds have spent half a century protesting that Eight Miles High was simply about being on an aeroplane. This song is not about crystal meth. He wrote it in 1965! The final verse where Jim says that he will 'drop a line' has nothing to do with coke or acid either. That's not what one does with the former, and the latter doesn't come in lines. He is promising to write a letter, kids, with pen and paper. It's a breakup song.

On an album where most of the songs could have been A-sides, this one ended up on the back of 'Light My Fire'. As an album track, it is a winner. The minor key feel and the stunning piano break make for one of The Doors' most haunting songs. Ray's piano and organ work give it a wonderful dreamlike quality.

This is another song from Jim's 1965 notebook and one that, I think, works well as a poem, even without the music. The opening lines evoke Romeo and Juliet:

Before you slip into unconsciousness
I'd like to have another kiss
Another flashing chance at bliss
Another kiss, another kiss

The story is that Jim Morrison spent the summer of 1965 breaking up with his high school girlfriend, Mary, and though this is not generally thought of as one of the great break-up albums, there is a case to be made by songs like this one. The narrator sounds sad but resigned. There are phrases like: 'Enclose me in your gentle rain' which are lovely and romantic before something colder like 'you'd rather cry, I'd rather fly'.

The title is likely drawn from one of the stories found in an ancient manuscript held by the Royal Irish Academy. Because of the fabric that the stories were recorded on, it is known as the Book of Dun Cow. One of the tales involves a hero, Conle, who is promised women and pleasure by a Druid woman if he will board a crystal ship. Jim uses the idea to suggest another life away from the woman he is breaking up with but promises to write when he returns. It's compelling because, though the song predates The Doors stardom, it sounds like the world he would soon arrive in.

'20th Century Fox' (Morrison, Manzarek, Kreiger, Densmore)

After three almost ridiculously superb tracks, this one is something of a comedown. The play on words in the title is funny, but the song doesn't go too far past a fairly standard picture of a hip young woman. It's a distant cousin of 'Like A Rolling Stone' except here, instead of the finest schools, she went to a 'manless' school. There are plenty of contenders for Jim Morrison's most inept phrase, but this is up there. Hopefully, he was trying to be funny. Coupling 'fashionably lean' with 'fashionably late' works well and the absence of clocks in her life is clever, but then we get something as tired as the 'Queen of Cool'. 'Elementary talk' is appealing, but the whole thing doesn't seem to say much when compared to 'Soul Kitchen' or 'The Crystal Ship'.

Lyrics aside, it's an agreeable mid-tempo garage rocker that probably went over well live at the Whisky. Robby's guitar intro and riff set the mood. His solo is probably the best one yet on the album. Paul Rothchild had the whole band stomping on a wooden platform to beef up the percussion in the chorus. It was covered almost immediately by Freddie 'Boom Boom' Cannon backed by The Strawberry Alarm Clock. Another notable cover is a 1976 version by Johnny Cougar. Cougar is, of course, John Mellencamp these days but was once a sort of American glam artist. The song appears on his *Chestnut Street Incident* album.

'Alabama Song' (Brecht, Weill)

I think this is one of The Doors finest moments. It's a cover, but unlike the more predictable stable of Chicago blues songs that they would draw on throughout their career, this one was first sung in Germany in 1930 as the Weimar Republic faltered and the Brown Shirts grew stronger. It comes from a chamber opera called *Rise And Fall Of The City Of Mahagonny,* a not so subtle critique of capitalism set in a fantastical America. The music was written by Kurt Weill with lyrics by Bertolt Brecht. These two also wrote *The Threepenny Opera,* which yielded 'Mack The Knife' and 'Pirate Jenny'. *The City Of Mahagonny* has never been quite as popular but continues to be produced periodically. The plot is, to be gentle, somewhat woolly, but the main characters all come together in a city of pleasure, Mahagonny, where eventually the main character, Jimmy, is executed for the capitalist crime of not having any money. Along the way, he meets a prostitute called Jenny. She sings 'Alabama Song' early in the opera as she leaves home in search of whiskey, boys, and money.

The Doors version came about when Ray suggested it and played a recording by the Austrian singer, Lotte Lenya, who was once married to Weill. There was a popular album of Lotte singing Kurt Weill songs and other Berlin Theatre numbers that had appeared in the late '50s. Readers of Bob Dylan's *Chronicles* will recall his enthusiasm for her version of 'Pirate Jenny' from *The Threepenny Opera*. It's possible that every household had this album. In any case, one would assume that Ray got the idea because they were playing a bar called Whisky A Go Go, and a song that opened with 'Oh show me the way to the next whiskey bar' might have seemed obvious. Supposedly, it was hearing them perform this song that convinced Jac Holzman to sign them to Elektra Records.

They don't deviate as much from Lotte Lenya as one might imagine. There are plenty of versions available to listen to online, and it is clear that The Doors modelled theirs on hers. Indeed, they seem to be revelling in the cabaret atmosphere. The band embraces the Oompa rhythm and Jim tells the story with Teutonic gusto. It sounds like a rock and roll song, albeit an offbeat one in every sense, but it is by no means a radical overall. There is something apposite about a band in LA recording a song from the Weimar era. Weimar Germany was an intensely creative period where conventional morality was up for discussion. The Doors were poised to ask similar questions.

'Light My Fire' (Morrison, Manzarek, Kreiger, Densmore)

I have an image in my mind of the prospective buyer of this book flipping to this very entry to see if I am a reliable guide to The Doors. What does he have to say about 'Light My Fire'? If he doesn't like it, I'm not interested!

To some extent, all hit songs share something of the zeitgeist of their moment, but Light My Fire might be one of the more obvious ones. Somehow, it manages to capture the emerging sexual revolution while, as we will see, also invoking the social one underway in 1967.

Rest assured, 'Light My Fire' is a song I love and have never grown tired of, despite its overwhelming popularity. I would suggest that one of the features of this track is that it never gets old. Right now, I am listening to the guitar solo and thinking that Robby Kreiger remains underrated as a lead player. I'm also hearing Densmore's light touch on the verses and the way that Ray Manzarek keeps pace with Jim throughout the song. Morrison, for his part, invents a sort of crooner rock and roll style that has been imitated endlessly ever since.

'Light My Fire' is one of the most compelling hits of the 1960s. It is darkly romantic, sophisticated, and great for dancing. It reached number one smack in the middle of the summer of love and turned The Doors into superstars exactly two years after Jim Morrison had ambled up to Ray Manzarek on Venice Beach with his collection of lyrics. This song was not in the book, of course, because Jim didn't write it. Robby Kreiger did.

During the band's early rehearsals in Ray Manzarek's rented beachfront house, Jim suggested that everyone go home and write a song. He advised them to invoke the natural elements, earth, air, water, and, of course, fire. It was good advice. Ray and John didn't turn up with anything, but Robby came back with a song about fire. He remembers it as pure folk rock when he played it for the band. There are clips of Robby on YouTube approximating his original idea, but, to my mind, they sound too much like Jose Feliciano's version to be credible. Whatever he had in mind, it was soon in the hands of Densmore, who suggested a Latin feel, and Ray, who came up with the timeless organ intro, which he has accredited to Bach and others over the years. Jim wrote the second verse where Robby's original ideas of romance somehow ended up as a 'funeral pyre.' The guitarist supposedly asked Jim why everything always came back to death. The singer just mumbled something like, 'sex, death, you know'. Clearly, he had done at least one literature course at university.

It's easy to dismiss the lyrics as nothing more than a series of rhymes for fire. But there is something unnerving about love becoming a funeral pyre and the mention of fire is, I believe, very significant. Fire was a regular feature of the news in America in this period. The summer of 1965 had seen the Watts Riots in LA, where blocks and blocks of the city had burned. There were riots in Chicago and Cleveland in 1966 and 1967, while this song was in the charts, and extensive rioting in Newark, Detroit, Harlem, Rochester, and several other cities. I'm not suggesting that Robby or Jim had riots in mind, but sometimes there are ideas in the air, and seeing cities burn would certainly put fire there. Some writers have suggested that footage of GIs burning Vietnamese villages in an attempt to flush out the elusive Vietcong might be in the mix as well. It was reportedly a great favourite of the young soldiers serving in South East Asia.

Amazingly, it wasn't the first single and was not scheduled to be one at all. It was too long. Dylan had pushed the envelope with 'Like A Rolling Stone' at six minutes. The album track of 'Light My Fire' was over seven. Like the Dylan song, it turned itself into a hit when DJs began to play it on the radio. Dylan was able to squeeze his whole song onto a 45, but it was an edited version of

'Light My Fire' that was released in April of 1967. The instrumental section was removed to the dismay of the band.

Elektra gave them each a present when the song hit number one. Jim got a 1967 Shelby Mustang, Ray and Robby requested some recording equipment, and John Densmore got a horse. It's interesting to reflect on The Doors had they not released 'Light My Fire'. They would have other hits, but their overall success would have been far more modest without this one. Would Jim have lived a bit longer? Would they have done more albums, been permitted to go in other directions? Who knows? 'Light My Fire' made them the number one act in America and life was never quite the same.

They appeared on the *Ed Sullivan Show* on 17 September 1967. It was their only appearance because although Jim had agreed to sing, 'Girl we couldn't get much better' and had done so in rehearsal, he sang the original line on the show. Ed was not pleased, and they were told they'd 'never do the *Sullivan Show*'. 'We just did', said Jim. It's worth noting that only nine months earlier, The Rolling Stones had agreed to change 'Let's Spend The Night Together' to 'Let's Spend Some Time Together.' Now Jim Morrison was singing about getting higher. A few months was a long time in the '60s, and the difference between the 'bad boy' Rolling Stones at the beginning of that year and Jim Morrison towards the end of it is significant. The Stones would catch up, of course, and then some, but there is no doubt that The Doors were a new kind of rock and roll band. There were others, of course, pulling on leather pants and growing out their mop tops, but not many were bagging number one records.

One of its many enduring qualities is the arrangement. The folk-rock song Robby imagined was something like The Leaves' 'Hey Joe'. Instead, it became one part Coltrane's 'Ole', a couple of parts Miles Davis' 'All Blue' with a mix of 3/4 and 4/4 time signatures, Manzarek's Bach noodlings, and a series of what John Densmore calls, 'interesting changes'. They are a long way from the garage here. Jim sounds like the lounge lizard king, crooning his way through the song with an almost arch tone. It's a remarkable performance cobbled together from several takes, done, like the rest of the record, live in the studio. A bass part by Larry Knetchel was overdubbed later but otherwise, what we hear is what they played. Ray has suggested that the bass line is based on Fats Domino's 'Blueberry Hill'. I would be very curious to hear an early live version of 'Light My Fire' to see what was added to the recording.

It has been covered hundreds of times. In fact, by the time Jose Feliciano's version appeared in 1968, it had already been done several times. Feliciano's take was a top ten hit in July of 1968 in the US and number one in Canada and Australia. I will now offer the possibly controversial opinion that his version is, to my ears, rather dull. The sweeping string sections make me feel like nothing so much as checking to make sure the button has been pressed for my floor. It was a huge success, so many people will not agree, but there you go. Some songs are not meant to be covered. I truly believe that this is one of them.

So the first side ends with one of the most famous singles of the era. Incredibly, the most astonishing music is yet to come.

Side Two
'Back Door Man' (Dixon, Burnett)

This might sound like an ancient blues standard, but it was only about seven years old when The Doors recorded it for their first album. It was written by Willie Dixon, the author of 'Hootchie Coochie Man', 'My Babe', 'Little Red Rooster', 'Spoonful', and many, many other songs that were recorded by the top shelf of Chicago blues artists and their younger British and American followers in the 1960s. The Rolling Stones, in particular, seemed partial to his compositions. 'Back Door Man' had been part of The Doors repertoire from the beginning and would remain a fixture of their live sets.

Willie Dixon was also the go-to double bass player for Chess Records artists and if you own records by Muddy Waters, Howlin' Wolf, Chuck Berry or Bo Diddley, you have tracks that he played on. Howlin' Wolf was the first to record 'Back Door Man' in 1960 for a release the following year on the flip side of 'Wang Dang Doodle'. Ray Manzarek would have certainly known the original, but it doesn't seem to be the basis for The Doors' version. In 1965, John Hammond Jr recorded the song for his second LP, *Big City Blues*. This album is considered a very early example of American blues rock and Robby Kreiger has suggested that it was this version that inspired The Doors.

The 'Back Door Man' in blues language refers to the kind of guy who spends his days with married women while their husbands are at work. The back door is his means of escape. An early reference appears in a song by Sara Martin, an early blues singer in the Bessie Smith mode. In her 1924 song, 'Strange Lovin Blues', she noted that 'every sensible woman got a back-door man.' Of course, the idea of the back door might have deeper and more serious implications. In the segregated southern US, African Americans were often instructed to use the back door or service entrance. Many blues lyrics contain coded references to racial discrimination.

The Doors make this song their own here. Using John Hammond Jr's arrangement as a starting point, they settle on a riff shared by Robby and Ray. Robby's guitar solo is understated and effective. Jim is in great voice here. His screams and moans build the erotic atmosphere of the song as he brags about his prowess. He drops Dixon's final verse about getting shot but adds some lines that contrast most men's pork and beans dinners with his appetite for chicken. It's all very suggestive and though this has become something of a blues standard, The Doors version has never lost its punch.

This was the song that they were playing when Jim became the first rock and roll star to be arrested mid-song on stage in New Haven on 9 December 1967. Before the show, Jim had been 'entertaining' a young female fan in a shower stall backstage when a police officer had approached him and told him to move along. Jim suggested the officer 'eat it' and was given a last chance. Jim said, 'last chance to eat it' and got maced. During 'Back Door Man', Jim recounted the incident in colourful language and was hauled away as the rest of the band played on. There is a soundless clip on YouTube of his arrest. The song was on the setlist of the band's final show with Morrison in New Orleans in 1971.

'I Looked At You' (Morrison, Manzarek, Kreiger, Densmore)

Ray Manzarek refers to this song as a 'silly little ditty' in his memoir. Mick Wall thinks it is a throwback to Rick & The Ravens. I disagree with both of them. On an album with 'Light My Fire', 'The End', 'Back Door Man' and 'End Of The Night', it's hard to get any attention, but 'I Looked At You' is cool. If somehow this album had flopped and this was an obscure garage song on a Pebbles compilation, you would be climbing over broken glass to find more material by this band. It's not a deep song, but there is more to it than meets the eye, or ear perhaps.

It is something of a throwback to 1964. It contains faint echoes of Dave Clark Five's 'Glad All Over' and The Beatles immediate post-mop-top period on the *Help!* album. It is, in other words, a brilliant '60s pop song with stunning guitar lines from Robby Kreiger. The secret hero of this album is Bruce Botnick, whose engineering skills are obvious on this song. Considering that most of these songs were done live on the floor, usually over an afternoon, the sound is remarkably sharp. It seems to have been the last song they recorded, so it may have been something of an afterthought. It's underrated, I believe, to the point that no one ever mentions it! It works very well on the second side as some light between the relative shade of 'Back Door Man' and the darkness of 'End Of The Night'.

Lyrically, it seems very slight. But is it? It could be that the narrator is talking about following the impulse of a chance meeting with a casual hook up – a sort of cousin to Dylan's 'If You Gotta Go'. On the other hand, there is the possibility of a mystical encounter here too. Listen to the song and imagine the narrator looking into a mirror. Now imagine the narrator is tripping. Yeah, different song altogether!

'End Of The Night' (Morrison, Manzarek, Kreiger, Densmore)

1967 was an incredible year for music in an incredible period. Along with *The Doors*, this was the year of Hendrix's first album, *Sgt. Pepper, Disraeli Gears, Forever Changes, Buffalo Springfield Again* and many others that would be immediately familiar to even the most casual listener. Very few of the many great bands of the era produced a dud in 1967. Whatever happened in 1965 to shift rock into a more sophisticated phase was still a vibrant force as bands went into the recording studio in 1966 or early 1967. As an experiment, try googling 'worst albums of 1967'. You will get nothing. Now try that with 1987. There are plenty of entries. My point is that The Doors' first album, despite perhaps the stiffest competition in any year since the dawn of the genre, remains a mainstay of any 'best of 1967' list. Or any 'best of' list at all. What sets it apart? Why is it so unique? Why is it arguably the best album of that stellar year?

'End Of The Night' would be a good place to start. This is early psychedelia that doesn't sound forced. Donovan's *Sunshine Superman* album from the same year is a top listen, but there is something deliberately dippy about it. It's affable and cool, in its way, but it is still dippy. *Sgt. Pepper* isn't dippy, but it does drift into a performative version of psychedelia at points. Hendrix is bold, but something like 'Manic Depression' is all about sonics. It's glorious, but it isn't subtle. 'End Of The Night' is subtle.

It's an early song for the band, one of the six recorded by Rick & The Ravens with Jim in the summer of 1965. That version, as noted, showed that the song was almost fully formed even at that early stage. But there has been one significant change. In that recording, the song opens with 'I took a journey to the end of the night'. On the album, Jim has altered it to 'Take the highway to the end of the night'. It's a far more evocative phrase. Instead of relating a personal story, the singer is making a suggestion. The highway image, which The Doors will return to again and again, places the song in the America of Sal Paradise, Tom Joad, and all of the other cowboys and pilgrims driving west into the setting sun.

Again, the production team is to be commended here. Everything from Kreiger's eerie slide guitar solo to Jim's chanting then shouting vocals are like fine crystal on this track. The space around the various elements – Robby's upward strummed chord, the main riff on the organ and so on – conveys the idea of night where sounds are framed by silence. Somehow it also makes a relatively brief song sound long. I was astonished to note the 2:49 running time. In my mind, this was a five-minute song, at least!

Like many others who came across this song as a teenager, I soon discovered that it was inspired by a book called *Journey To The End Of The Night* by the French writer Louis-Ferdinand Celine. It was published in 1932 and is considered by many to be one of the key novels of the 20th century. It's not an easy or pleasant read, but the main character's alienation, restlessness, and general disillusionment will be familiar to readers of Henry Miller, the Beats, JD Salinger, and Joseph Heller. Jim Morrison's literary tastes tended towards the twentieth-century avant-garde, but there is another more direct reference in this song. 'Some are born to sweet delight' is a line from William Blake's poem, 'Auguries of Innocence'. Blake, of course, provided the band's name, so it is interesting to see him quoted in this song.

Blake's poem suggests that every cruelty against innocence 'augurs' badly for the world. Morrison seems to be going somewhere else in this song. He seems to be suggesting that the pure delight might be in Celine's night world and that knowledge is attained there. Blake talks about 'poor souls who dwell in night', but Jim doesn't seem so sure. My sense is that like Dylan, who also found this poem inspiring, Morrison was attracted to the cadence of the lines rather than

Blake's message. Whatever he had in mind, 'End Of The Night' remains one of The Doors finest moments.

'Take It As It Comes' (Morrison, Manzarek, Kreiger, Densmore)

Another sleeper on the album, squeezed in between 'End Of The Night' and 'The End', 'Take It As It Comes' is a necessary interlude. 'Specialise in having fun', says Jim here. The song begins, like The Byrds' recent Pete Seeger cover, 'Turn! Turn! Turn!', with Ecclesiastes 3:4's famous sequence of 'a time to be born, a time to die....' Morrison starts with 'time to live, time to lie', which is an interesting twist. There is some idea that this song was written with the Maharishi in mind, and indeed, the title does sound like something he might have said. Robby, Ray, and John met at a TM session, so it is possible that the 'take it easy' sentiment came from that source. That said, according to John Densmore, Jim wasn't much interested in Eastern thought. My take is that this is another mirror song. Jim, except in rare instances, is not a confessional style songwriter. However, he does seem to use the second person in a manner that might indicate he is addressing himself.

Ray Manzarek said that, musically, the song resembles Thelonious Monk's 'Straight, No Chaser'. His organ solo is another Bach inspired high point on the album, but Monk is harder to discern here. What might be more obvious is Robby's love of Spanish guitar in the chorus' A minor chord progression. The section at the end where Jim sings over the bass and drums is magnificent as well, particularly when the full band comes back in and he raises his voice.

The Ramones' surprisingly reverential cover is a good place to hear the garage punk underbelly of this song. It is essentially a pop song, but the changes and Manzarek's eerie organ solo give it the uneasy atmosphere that set this band apart so strikingly from so many of their contemporaries. Despite the positive lyrics, there is nothing giddy here. The band delivers this song with such conviction and self-assurance that, again, it is hard to believe that it was part of their first record.

'The End' (Morrison, Manzarek, Kreiger, Densmore)

On what would be their last night at Whisky A Go Go in August of 1966, three of The Doors were nervously watching the door. The problem was that their lead singer, Jim Morrison, hadn't turned up. After a couple of months, the band had gone from obscurity to something like a cult phenomenon for the incredibly hip and/or the incredibly weird. People were talking about The Doors and most of them were focussing their discussion on Jim. It's easy to forget that The Doors would not have initially appeared hip to the Whisky crowd. They were scruffy beatniks from Venice and Jim seemed to have no concept of what a pop singer was supposed to do. Sure, he sang the songs, but he also read poems, told stories and jokes, screamed, and lay down on the stage. The last time anyone had seen a guy like this, there had been bongoes involved. But he was more than a dubious poet. There was something about him, and everyone was trying to get a closer look. The band was pretty good too and you could dance to them.

But the minutes ticked by with no sign of Jim. A decision was made to seek him out at his man cave in the Tropicana Motel around the corner. They arrived to find him under the bed, tripping wildly. They somehow talked him out from his hiding spot and coaxed him back to the Whisky. Once on stage, he managed well enough. He sang, he ducked invisible bats, he glared at people, and, safe to say, nobody noticed a thing.

They had, for some time, been performing a song called 'The End'. It was a breakup song, probably another written for Mary, his high school girlfriend. At least for the first verse. After that, it went somewhere entirely different and at the Whisky, Jim had taken to using it as a backdrop to various poems and ramblings. This evening, after emerging from under the bed on acid, he went somewhere new.

Ray Manzarek heard the now-famous line, 'the killer awoke before dawn' and thought, 'oh boy, where are we going with this?' Down the hall, it turned out, to visit the various members of his family. By the time Jim got to his mother's room, the Whisky, filled with people wasted on a wide variety of substances, had gone very, very, quiet. He had threatened to kill his father. What was he going to say to his mother? Wait a minute. Ancient face? Greek Drama. This is Oedipus! Ray, well-read fellow that he was, knew what was coming and must have braced himself. When Jim delivered the line about his mother, the place went nuts. The owner was incensed and fired them on the spot. In this postmodern world where nothing shocks us anymore, it might seem quaint, but this was 1966 and one did not proposition one's mother in a song on stage in a nightclub. The residency was over. They started recording this album a couple of days later.

For people of my generation, 'The End' will be forever associated with Francis Ford Coppola's 1979 film, *Apocalypse Now*. It opens the film in one of the most haunting sequences in cinema history. I have already discussed the cinematic elements in The Doors music. Somehow Coppola must have noted that quality in 'The End' and recognised how it could set the stage for this epic film. The song has nothing to do with the Vietnam War, but you would be forgiven for assuming that it did when the lines 'Desperately in need / Of some stranger's hand / In a desperate land' float over an image mirroring Martin Sheen's face, that will appear later in the film as a large Laotian carving. Similarly, the third verse, which begins with 'Lost in a Roman wilderness of pain', plays over scenes of burning villages and helicopters, taking on a whole new meaning. Coppola uses the instrumental section after the Oedipal sequence from the original take, with Jim muttering about what is going to happen to mother and father to frame Sheen's tai chi wig out in the Saigon hotel room, but finishes up on 'all the children are insane' as Captain Willard embarks on his mission. The blue bus sequence turns up in the dramatic ending where Willard terminates Kurtz's command with extreme prejudice.

The Oedipal bit never appears but is, of course, heavily implied as Willard walks out to kill Kurtz. The 'summer rain' falling gently on the young soldier, Sam Bottoms' Lance Johnson, in the closing minutes is implied as well. Both sections of the film are unforgettable but would be much less so without this song. Oh, and by the way, Francis Ford Coppola went to UCLA film school in the early sixties and knew both Ray and Jim.

But back in 1967, before the fictional events in *Apocalypse Now* had even taken place, The Doors were recording the song that had got them fired from their most recent regular gig. Seeing as this was no more than a week after the events described above, there is the distinct possibility that what was captured in the studio was not a definitive version, if one ever existed, but a work in progress. Certainly, the various live versions that followed show that the song continued to evolve in Jim's mind.

Supposedly only two takes were done and the one on the album is the second. Once again, it was all recorded live. It begins with some lovely Spanish guitar work from Robby as he settles into the hypnotic, almost raga style riff. His guitar work is astonishing. The bends and arpeggios after the second verse set the stage for the 'roman wilderness'. John Densmore's considerable talents are on show here, too, as the drums move melodically through the song. Ray fills it out with restrained organ sections as Jim works his way through the story. Morrison's delivery is stunning. He sings the verses with great conviction and clarity before performing the Oedipal sequence like the great actor he might have been in a different life. The final raga sequence is punctuated by Jim chanting 'fuck' percussively. This was, naturally, buried in the mix by Bruce Botnick on the original release in 1967 but restored on the 1999 remastered version.

But what does it all mean? It seems like fragments of a story when read on the page. The narrator leaves his girlfriend and embarks on a journey that takes him to a series of fantastical landscapes, including a 'Roman wilderness of pain' where 'all the children are insane'. Many have suggested that this is a comment on the emerging counterculture, and it may be, but this isn't how Jim approached his writing. Later I will address songs that are referencing specific events, but my sense of this original batch, most of which were drawn from the journals he was writing in 1965 or earlier, is that they are journeys through Jim's imaginative landscape rather than social commentary. As with 'End Of The Night', this is a writer experimenting with a variety of ideas and approaches. 'The King's Highway', 'the blue bus', and the number seven in the length of the snake have variously been explained as the Camino Real (Road Royal) that runs through California, the Santa Monica bus system, and all the sevens (angels, churches, seals, etc.) in the *Book of Revelation*. It's all possible, but in reality, it seems to be more like a series of images in a cut-up narrative like one finds in William Burroughs' novels. The images are dreamlike but rich with implication. Weird scenes inside the goldmine, indeed! In the goldmine of Jim's imagination, there is also a family home where 'the killer' awakes before dawn and puts on a mask, signifying Greek drama, before visiting the rooms of his brother and sister. We assume that they are murdered but it isn't stated. He then 'walks on down the hall' to those of his parents. It hasn't escaped people's notice that Jim is describing his own family. He had a brother and a sister and, of course, a mother and father. I will let biographers speculate further!

The song ends by once again becoming a breakup song. It is as though the narrator has, while finishing the relationship, descended into a psychological underworld – like Orpheus perhaps – and returned to say the final parting words.

There are two other stories about this song. One is true, one isn't. The one that isn't true is Ray Manzarek's colourful tale of Jim throwing Bruce Botnick's portable television through the control booth window in the recording studio. Ray says that Bruce had brought it in to watch Sandy Koufax pitch for the Los Angeles Dodgers in the 1966 World Series. A problem right away is that the 1966 World Series took place in October of that year, by which time the album was being mixed. The idea was that Jim objected to the TV being on in the studio while they were recording 'The End' and smashed it. Bruce says he was watching Koufax pitch and that Jim did object to the TV being on. Botnick apologized and turned it off. Later, Jim bumped into it and knocked it on the floor. According to the engineer, he still had the television in 2017 and it was still working. Incidentally, Sandy Koufax owned the Tropicana Motel, where Jim was living at the time.

The true story is that after they recorded 'The End' and packed up for the day, Jim wandered over to the Catholic church across the street and, as he was wont to do, dropped acid. Then he returned to the studio. Somehow, he ended up inside, naked and covered in retardant from the fire extinguisher. Elektra Records paid for the damages.

'The End' is one of The Doors' finest moments. All of the elements that make their catalogue so compelling are here. It has a cinematic quality that was noted and employed by Francis Ford Coppola and a tantalising series of literary allusions. Musically, it is Robby at one of his most inventive moments and Ray at his intuitive best. It also makes the case, one that should be made more often, that John Densmore is one of the great rock drummers. Ending your first album with a song called 'The End' could be construed in many ways but, as we will see, 'The End' was only the beginning.

Strange Days (1967)

Recorded: May to August 1967 at Sunset Sound Recorders, Hollywood, California
Released: September 1967
Label: Elektra
Producer: Paul Rothchild
Engineer: Bruce Botnick
Additional musicians: Doug Lubahn (bass guitar)
Running Time: 35:25
Highest Chart Position: US: 3 UK: Did not chart

Eve Babitz, the author of *Eve's Hollywood* and an early girlfriend of Jim
Morrison, put it best when she wondered what was left to say after 'this is
the end'. If there was ever going to be a difficult second album, it was going
to be the one after The Doors' debut. Someone, maybe David Crosby, once
said that you have ten years to write your first album and ten minutes to write
the second. Since the dawn of popular music, acts have had to balance the
promotion of a successful first release with the creation of a follow-up. In the
sixties, bands would immediately begin to tour heavily to support the sales of
an album. They would go on television, sit for interviews, and deal with the
pressures of sudden fame. Rock and roll is littered with one-hit wonders and
disappointing second albums.

Strange Days isn't one of them.

Many consider this to be their best album. Jim Morrison was one of them. In
several interviews, he suggested that it built on the ideas of the first album. Its
producer, Paul Rothchild, later said that he thought it was their best album and
that it continued from where the debut left off without losing any momentum.
He also felt that despite the wider sonic landscape on the album, it was not
overproduced.

One of the reasons that *Strange Days* doesn't seem to feature any typical
'difficult second album' characteristics may be explained by the timeline.
Recording started about a month after the January release of The Doors album.
It was recorded in short bursts throughout the first half of 1967 and released in
September. This wise move on someone's part to capture that original energy
before it dissipated is something more record companies should have done
in that period. The Doors hadn't been exhausted by the post 'Light My Fire'
storm or spent months touring when they started this record. They had no
idea how their first album would be received, so they are, in a sense, still the
'band from Venice', hungry to make it on *Strange Days*. They were also still
working from Jim's original notebooks, according to Rothchild and others, so
these songs were mined from the same vein as those on the first album. In fact,
'Moonlight Drive', the song that Jim sang to Ray during their famous Venice
Beach encounter, appears on this album, along with the title track, which can
be heard on the *London Fog* album. 'My Eyes Have Seen You', a song from the
1965 demo, also appears.

The album was recorded, like the first one, at Sunset Sound Recorders, but Bruce Botnick had procured an 8-track 3M tape recorder which opened up possibilities for the band in the studio. There is some question of when this change was made, but it seems to have been in place for the bulk of the recording dates. It was certainly there by the time they recorded 'Moonlight Drive' in April, according to the notes on the tape box. He also obtained, at some stage of the recording, an acetate of The Beatles' *Sgt. Pepper* album, which he played for Paul Rothchild and the band. It wouldn't be until *The Soft Parade* that Rothchild would attempt something deliberately conceptual, but it is clear that The Doors and their production team felt as though they now had permission to pursue an expanded (a word used by both Paul Rothchild and Jim to describe the album) sound. It's probably not an exaggeration to emphasise the importance of The Beatles' *Sgt. Pepper's Lonely Hearts Club Band* to the band. For The Doors themselves, it was the sense that they could go as far out as they pleased. For the producer and the engineer, it was a new paradigm. This wasn't just a matter of creating three minutes of radio-friendly fun anymore. The pop LP had become an art form unto itself. Brian Wilson had famously responded to the challenge of *Revolver* with *Pet Sound*s. The Beatles had returned fire with Pepper. Some American bands, notably Frank Zappa and The Mothers Of Invention, joined the fray in 1967. Elektra Records seemed drawn to the emerging form. Love's *Forever Changes*, Tim Buckley's *Goodbye And Hello*, and the now largely forgotten debut by Clear Light all fit in here. The beginning point of American prog rock is best left for late-night discussions. The existence of American prog alone is an argument starter. If it does exist, there is a case to be made for *Strange Days* as a possible starting point. Why not *Absolutely Free* or *After Bathing At Baxters*? Why indeed not *Pet Sounds*? The case to be made has to do with a particular instrument employed on the title track. I'm not suggesting that The Doors should be regarded as a prog act, but they might have contributed something very important to the genre on this record.

It's worth noting that it was during the recording of *Strange Days* that The Doors began to play regularly in San Francisco. The San Francisco scene was very different from that of LA at the time. The band played their first gigs after the release of the first album at the Fillmore over several weekends in early 1967. They attended but did not play at the Human Be-In in February and headlined the Avalon Ballroom in early March. They had a somewhat uneasy relationship with San Francisco. Their shows were well received, and they were quickly headlining gigs at the Fillmore. But The Doors were not a hippie band, and something about their dark version of acid, and life in general, never seemed quite right to the tastemakers in San Francisco. They were not invited to the Monterey Pop Festival, and when they became popular, were all too quickly dismissed by the San Francisco 'counterculture'. Relations with The Grateful Dead were never particularly good either. Ray Manzarek once asked Ron Pigpen McKernan if, instead of hauling his own Vox organ up on stage, could he just use The Dead's. Ron said simply, 'no one touches The Dead's stuff'. Ray protested that it was an identical instrument and was told the same thing again. Later Ray was amused that someone called Pigpen wouldn't let him touch HIS stuff. Jerry Garcia, who displayed a real loathing for The Doors in later interviews, called Morrison's moves 'pure Mick Jagger worship'. At least he was moving.

Side One
'Strange Days' (Morrison, Manzarek, Kreiger, Densmore)
The title track is one of the band's great moments and immediately shuts down any idea of second album jitters. It is the perfect response to Eve Babitz's question. After the end? Well, strange days have found us.

Some listeners at the time interpreted it as being about the band's newfound fame. In fact, 'Strange Days' was recorded, according to some sources, two days after 'Light My Fire' was released as a single in April of 1967. It is also on the London Fog recordings from 1966, suggesting that the lyrics date back to Jim's prolific summer of 1965. Setlists for the Whisky A Go Go shows are hard to track down, but as the song was part of their repertoire at London Fog, it can be assumed that it remained part of it for the remainder of 1966. It was played live at The Scene in New York in June 1967 but then more or less disappears from their shows.

I promised that I would offer some evidence of this album's importance to the prog canon. Here it is: There is an album on Elektra Records that was recorded at about the same time as *Strange Days* called *The Zodiac: Cosmic Sounds,* which is almost the definition of a lost classic. It is essentially a showcase for the 'synthesizer', an instrument invented by Robert Moog in 1964. Jac Holzman, the owner of Elektra Records, had the idea of creating an 'electronic' pop album using the Moog. The concept was the twelve signs of the zodiac. A singer called Cyrus Faryar narrated a series of zodiac inspired reflections over a surprisingly melodic backdrop. It's worth hearing. The rhythm section of Hal Blaine and Carol Kaye give it a driving mid-sixties groove. What is most interesting for our purposes is how much it sounds like The Doors. It would be very easy to mistake Faryar's baritone vocals for Jim's, and the keyboard work is even more similar at points, particularly in the Virgo section.

At some stage, Paul Rothchild invited Paul Beaver, an early embracer of synths, to put Jim's vocal track on the song 'Strange Days' through the Moog. He then mixed the result with Jim's straight vocal and added some delay and reverb. The result is that Jim sounds like he is singing in a dreamscape somewhere. It makes the song. The 'strangeness' is underscored by a voice that sounds distant and obscure. This was virtually the first use of a synthesizer in Rock and Roll but not, of course, the last. Elektra bought a Moog when they eventually moved into their own studio, but the instrument never again appeared on a Doors album. A guitarist called George Harrison visited

35

Elektra Studios at some stage and showed a lot of interest in the Moog. Paul Beaver was involved in the production of the Magical Mystery Tour recordings later that year. There has been some suggestion that The Beatles were very interested in The Doors.

According to the engineer Bruce Botnick, Paul Beaver later climbed Mt. McKinley to check in with an alien spacecraft that was scheduled to refuel there. It was the sixties.

The bass line in 'Strange Days' shares something with Them's 'Gloria', and betrays the song's 1966 garage roots in The Doors' early period. It is played by the man who turned down the bass chair in The Doors but played on many tracks. Doug Lubahn was a founding member of another Elektra act, Clear Light, whose only album is well worth hearing. The band featured Dallas Taylor, later of CSNY on drums, and actor Cliff De Young on vocals. Lubahn's bass work with Clear Light is outstanding, and it is interesting to speculate on what he might have brought to The Doors as a full-time member. His bass line in this song is central, which might be one reason it didn't become part of their live set. As always, Ray provides eerie colour on the organ, particularly on the memorable descending pattern that opens the song.

These are some of Jim Morrison's most intriguing lyrics as he describes a surreal party that some have suggested is a metaphor for the emerging counterculture in California. Jim Morrison was well-read enough in poetry that the influence of T.S. Eliot's 'The Love Song Of J. Alfred Prufrock' might not be out of the question here. The line, 'Strange eyes fill strange rooms', might have some link to the room in Eliot's poem where the women come and go. The line that follows: 'Voices will signal their tired end', seems almost certainly influenced by Eliot's famous ending, 'Till Human voices wake us, and we drown.' Others have noted the influence of Eliot's masterwork 'The Wasteland' on Morrison's writing, so it is likely that he was aware of this equally famous one as well.

'You're Lost Little Girl' (Morrison, Manzarek, Kreiger, Densmore)

There are, to put it mildly, a lot of tall tales surrounding this band. Along with all the 'shaman' descriptions, there are a series of vivid oft-told stories which may be true, partly true, or completely fictional. Oliver Stone's film treated most of them like the gospel truth, including this one:

Apparently, Paul Rothchild had the rather dubious idea that Jim Morrison's vocals could be enhanced if a particular sex act was to be performed on him during the recording. According to John Densmore, there was some talk about hiring a professional. Instead, Jim's girlfriend, Pamela Courson volunteered and headed into the vocal booth. The story gets a bit hazy here. No one seems to know what happened and Densmore says, rather hilariously, that they 'went with a later take.' Ray Manzarek, who was never one to shy away from a good story, doesn't mention it in his memoir. If I was to guess, I'd say it was a joke that grew into something more as the years wore on. That said, Jim Morrison, as we have already seen, was capable of just about anything.

This is one of Robby Kreiger's songs. The lyrics are pretty slight, but Jim manages to invest them with more meaning than they have on paper. The music writer Barney Hoskyn called this song 'psychedelic Sinatra', which is pretty apt. Like Frank, one of Jim's great strengths as a singer is to locate the weight in even the lightest of lyrics. Listen to the emphasis on words like 'lost', 'who', and 'impossible'. According to John Densmore, the band talked seriously about pitching the song to Frank Sinatra. They thought maybe he could sing it to his much younger new wife, Mia Farrow.

Once again, Doug Lubahn plays a substantial role. The song starts with a walking bass line before being joined by a neat little reverb-laden riff from Kreiger. The organ appears at the beginning of the first verse but backs off during the chorus. Robby's guitar solo is wonderful, if too brief.

Sometimes a cover version can reveal a song in unexpected ways. Siouxsie And The Banshees' recording of it is a good example. Without doing anything radical to the melody, she finds an almost German cabaret element in it and ends up sounding a bit like Jim's old buddy, Nico, fronting the Velvet Underground.

'Love Me Two Times' (Morrison, Manzarek, Kreiger, Densmore)

This is one of the great songs by this band and familiar to many people who might not otherwise know much about The Doors. It was the second single from the album and a frequent live song that featured in the last show ever for the original quartet in New Orleans in 1970. Robby Kreiger wrote both the music and the lyrics of this one, and, like many of these songs, it was recorded for the first album but excluded from the final version.

The wonderful blues riff that defines it was adapted from a song called 'Southbound' by John Koerner. It appeared on an LP collection called *The Blues Project* (that predated the band by that name), which featured folk artists like Dave Van Ronk, Geoff Muldaur and others performing blues songs. Like many aspiring guitarists of the period, Robby Kreiger learned to play several blues riffs by working his way through this record. John Koerner is largely forgotten these days but was a very early influence on Bob Dylan and made several brilliant albums in a trio with Dave Ray and Tony Glover. Later he ended up on Elektra Records in a duo with Willie Murphy.

'Love Me Two Times' was inspired, according to Robby, by young men leaving for Vietnam, and when considered in this light, the 'once for tomorrow, once just for today' takes on a more serious tone. Of course, in the hands of Jim Morrison, the song was suggestive to the point that it was predictably banned here and there. Ray Manzarek calls it a great blues-rock song about multiple orgasms.

It's also perhaps an unusual great blues rock song in that it features a harpsichord solo. Some accounts say that Ray is playing the clavichord, but his memoir is pretty clear. He says the harpsichord 'worked like a champ'.

The Doors would certainly continue to play blues songs, particularly on their later albums, but it is Ray's use of a baroque instrument that makes this one so distinctive.

'Unhappy Girl' (Morrison, Manzarek, Kreiger, Densmore)

This is another song that was recorded but not used on the first album. It was the final song recorded for *Strange Days* in August of 1967. It was the flip side of the first single, 'People Are Strange', and is, as they say, a fan favourite. It falls into the psychedelic Sinatra camp, with some people suggesting that it sounds like an acid-soaked 'My Funny Valentine'. The lyrics are not particularly profound, though Morrison does come up with 'prison of your own device', which presumably the future members of The Eagles filed away for later use. The 'unhappy girl' is 'playing solitaire' in a metaphorical jail cell. The narrator tells her not to miss her chance to 'swim in mystery'. Like 'Break On Through' and others, there is a sense of seeking freedom from psychological restraints. Jim Morrison, rather wittily, later described the band as 'erotic politicians'. In the late sixties, when the idea of freedom was at the centre of the popular discourse, The Doors added their own slightly dark version with this and many other songs.

One of the interesting features of this song is Ray's piano part. According to his memoir, *Light My Fire*, he wrote out the entire part backwards and somehow played along to a tape of the band which had been turned over and run from the end to the beginning. Then his part, which he had played backwards, was itself run backwards so that it was forward. Confused? Imagine how Ray felt! It's quite effective and as John Densmore says, it sounds percussive. The organ part is interesting as well. On the live recording from March 1967, available on the *Live At The Matrix 1967* album, the song opens with a quasi-classical organ solo. On both, Robby's subtle slide work adds to the surreal atmosphere of the song.

'Horse Latitudes' (Morrison, Manzarek, Kreiger, Densmore)

This was one of Jim Morrison's early poems, a high school effort that must have given his English teacher some pause as he or she marked papers after dinner. It's an astounding piece of writing and remains one of The Doors' great moments.

The horse latitudes are the subtropical regions between 30 and 50 degrees on both sides of the equator. For sailors, it was the part of a long journey where the winds were often calm, and the trip slowed down considerably. No one is entirely clear on why they are called the 'horse' latitudes, but there are several theories. Young Jim went, predictably, with the darkest. There is some idea that as the ship slowed down and water grew scarce, horses would be jettisoned into the sea as a way of cutting down on water consumption. Considering that the horses would have been part of the cargo, this seems a bit unlikely, but Jim apparently was struck by the idea of horses being driven from the deck of a galleon into the sea.

The poem starts off describing the conditions of the latitudes with a nod to Coleridge's 'thousand thousand slimy things', with the idea that the still sea 'breeds tiny monsters'. Then he describes the moment when the horse is pushed into the sea and how they drown. His description is filled with moving details – the stiff green gallop in the water, the heads up with poise before what he terms the 'nostril agony' of drowning. It's a vivid and terrifying picture.

Jim's delivery is utterly captivating and another good example of his ability to create drama with his voice. Like Sinatra, he is essentially a storyteller and whatever the limitations of his singing voice may have been, he is almost peerless among sixties rock and roll singers in this regard. They are rarely mentioned in the same breath, but as a singer, Leonard Cohen might be a better comparison than Jagger or Lennon. 'Horse Latitudes' is the first of several spoken word pieces that appeared on Doors albums in his lifetime.

But there is more than just Jim's voice on this track. The use of electronic effects and other ambient noises build the drama of the piece. Ray Manzarek says that he thought they created something like the sound of a nineteenth-century ship in the Sargasso Sea. Ray played the piano strings with a mallet, and various other instruments, including a Coke can were employed. But Bruce Botnick is the true auteur here. According to a 2017 interview in Shindig magazine, he recorded tape hiss and then added echo. He then recorded it again, feeding the tape through the analogue machine by hand, thus varying the speed. It has been widely described as an example of musique concrete, the creation of sounds using electronic means. It is a good example of how The Doors expanded their sound on this album. According to John Densmore, some members of the Jefferson Airplane were present while Jim recorded his part in total darkness. They were suitably impressed.

Jim Morrison's debt to the Beat writers is clear both in the structure and his performance. 'Horse Latitudes' is arguably the first spoken-word piece to appear on a more or less mainstream rock and roll record. Certainly, by the time this album was mixed, the band had a number one hit with 'Light My Fire'. The inclusion of 'Horse Latitudes' demonstrates clearly that The Doors were not prepared, at this stage, to rest on their laurels. I will not claim that 'Horse Latitudes' set the stage for hip hop, but it certainly carved out some space for spoken word in popular music.

This is not covered very often, but a Doors cover band from Russia, al Alabama's version on YouTube, is worth watching if for nothing else than the confused couple on the dancefloor wondering what has happened.

'Moonlight Drive' (Morrison, Manzarek, Kreiger, Densmore)

This is the foundational Doors song, the beginning of the whole franchise. It was, according to Manzarek, the song that Jim Morrison sang to him on the beach at Venice in the summer of 1965. It was on the demo tape made soon after that meeting. It was also, apparently, the first song that the four final members played together when Robby Kreiger joined the band after the departure of Ray's brothers. He played slide guitar on that occasion and Jim fell in love with the sound immediately. It came and went on their live setlist but was played at least once on their final tour in 1970. It's a special song in the Doors catalogue because somewhere in the lyrics is whatever it was that caught Ray Manzarek's attention that day.

Moonlight has long been a mainstay of romantic poetry and popular song. From Shakespeare's 'How sweet the moonlight sleeps upon the bank' from *The Merchant of Venice* to Billie Holiday's 'What a Little Moonlight Can Do', the moon and its reflection have been associated with passion. Many have suggested that 'Moonlight Drive' is a song about death or a proposed double suicide, but a close reading will reveal that lovers are not in the water but nearby in a car, 'Parked beside the ocean / On our moonlight drive'. Later he notes that they are 'by the ocean side'. It is a classic seduction song where the narrator invites his lover to join him for a metaphorical swim towards the moon, presumably in the back seat. The imagery is erotic rather than ominous and the invitation to 'drown' is not literal. This is classic early Jim Morrison, romantic with the ever-present Nietzschean imperative to break out or transcend.

The arrangement underlines the playful lyrics. It's a series of fairly standard pop changes punctuated by Robby's slide work. This was a song that they had been playing nightly for more than a year and had recorded before as one of the early demos and for their first album. I've always wondered why they didn't release it as an A-side. It sounds polished and radio-friendly. It is on the flip side of 'Love Me Two Times'.

Side Two

'People Are Strange' (Morrison, Manzarek, Kreiger, Densmore)
This remains one of the best-loved songs by this band. It has a timeless quality that transcends any idea of 'classic rock' or the 'sixties'. When the Echo And The Bunnymen version appeared at the beginning of Joel Schumacher's 1987 film, *The Lost Boys*, there was no sense that this was an 'old' song. It caught the sense of teenage alienation in Reagan's America as accurately as it did in 1967.

There is an unfinished aspect to many of Morrison's lyrics that is both exhilarating in that it captures his creative imagination in action, and slightly frustrating when the ideas don't seem fully developed. 'People Are Strange' is, I believe, an example of a lyric that is fully formed. The story is that he wrote it quickly while watching the sunset from somewhere in Laurel Canyon in 1967. This is one of two songs on this album that don't seem to have come from his original 1965 burst of lyrics. It doesn't appear to have been recorded for the first album either, unlike most of the other songs. This is, therefore, a 'new' song on this record. If this is true, his writing has already shifted to a less ornate style. There is a simple power in lines like 'streets are uneven when you are down' and a curious ambiguity in the faces that 'come out in the rain'. Robby Kreiger, who wrote the music, said that the song grew out of a period of depression for Jim. John Densmore notes that, to him, the song sounded personal. If that is the case, it is perhaps a rare glimpse of Morrison's actual state of mind in the period. Like many writers, he appeared to have written in character mainly. This may be a notable, and highly successful, exception.

The production is masterful. The cinematic aspect of The Doors is on show here with Densmore's loping beat and Kreiger's mournful lead fills. Ray Manzarek's slightly off-centre piano solo evokes an old silent film soundtrack to match the gothic elements in the lyrics.

This was the first single from the album. It did not quite reach the *Billboard* Top Ten, though it went to number one in Canada. The version on *Live At The Matrix 1967* probably predates the recording but sounds more or less like the finished product. It doesn't seem to have featured in their live shows much after 1967. It was one of a handful of songs they got through before Jim was arrested onstage in New Haven late in that year. The clip of them playing it on Ed Sullivan is well worth watching. The 'Light My Fire' performance is very famous, but they also performed this song that night. If you can ignore the garish doors hanging on the set behind him, Jim delivers this song with great conviction and care.

As mentioned above, the song was revived by Echo and The Bunnymen, a band often compared to The Doors at the time, for the soundtrack of The Lost Boys. The film, a rather witty reflection on teenage life, pays tribute to Jim by placing a large poster of his image in the cave where the adolescent vampires live. As far as Doors covers go, this is a pretty good one. Mac swings the vocal line slightly to make it his own. It isn't a radical rereading, and the very Doors-like organ solo is an interesting touch.

'My Eyes Have Seen You' (Morrison, Manzarek, Kreiger, Densmore)

This is not a particularly well-known song, though it was apparently the second song that Jim sang to Ray on the beach that day. It was also recorded, in full garage glory, for the 1965 demo before Robby had joined the band. It was part of their live sets in 1967 but otherwise seems to be the very definition of an album track. That is not to say that it is 'filler' on this record. A quick search online reveals great affection for this song.

The version on the album retains some of the garage energy of the demo version but has evolved into a more psychedelic outing. Robby's guitar solo is reasonably heavy and something about Jim chanting 'television skies' makes it sound a bit punk rock. It's a cool song that lifts the tempo agreeably between 'People Are Strange' and 'I Can't See Your Face'.

The lyrics are clever. It was supposedly written while Jim was living with a friend on the top floor of an apartment building in Venice. He moved out onto the roof and spent his evenings tripping and writing in his journal. The song wittily evokes the first line from 'The Battle Hymn of the Republic', 'mine eyes have seen the glory of the coming of the lord'. It might seem like another psychedelic ode to his high school girlfriend but instead makes more sense as a song about LA itself. 'My eyes have seen you free from disguise / Gazing on a city under television skies'. The 'endless roll' makes sense if you picture an aerial shot of this flat city at night. It's not a spoiler to note that Jim Morrison will write about Los Angeles again on albums to come, so this may just be an early reflection on his adopted town.

'I Can't See Your Face In My Mind' (Morrison, Manzarek, Kreiger, Densmore)

Paul Rothchild is one of the great producers, no question, but he had some cringe-worthy moments in the studio. The story here is that he turned out all of the lights for the recording of this one and used some guided meditation to get them in the mood. 'Imagine you are in a Japanese garden....' So far, so good, a calm Zen setting ... '...with a beautiful girl.' Geez. The finished product, another lesser-known Doors track, works out pretty well despite the dark dose of sixties mush the band was subjected to while creating it.

This is another song where the expansion of their sound is revealed. The marimba adds some mysterious colour to the somewhat opaque lyrics and, in a creative use of the 8- tracks, one of John Densmore's cymbal recordings is run backwards. It's a quiet song but one of the more psychedelic moments on the album. Robby employs his slide, gently echoing the vocal line. Jim is in fine lysergic crooner mode here and all in all, this is something of a little gem.

They didn't play it live more than a few times in 1967, but the version on *Live At The Matrix 1967* reveals that, before the Japanese garden etc., it was a slightly more upbeat song. That live version features the organ and gives the listener an idea of what it might have sounded like as a more standard Doors song.

I'm afraid you are on your own with the lyrics here. Like the band in the dark studio, I'm having enough trouble just picturing a 'carnival dog', let alone working out the metaphorical implications of one. Someone in an online forum rather charitably referred to the image as 'Joycean'. Ditto perhaps for 'insanity's horse', although this might be an oblique reference to the night sky. As loathe as I am to consign his lyrics to the usual, 'this is about an acid trip' explanation, it may apply here. In any case, it might also be the best Doors' song you've either never heard or never noticed.

'When The Music's Over' (Morrison, Manzarek, Kreiger, Densmore)

The Doors' arrival in San Francisco for their first gig there was only a couple of days after the release of their first album. By that point, San Francisco was a mecca for the emerging counterculture. The Grateful Dead held court at a large house on Ashbury St., a short walk from the hippie ground zero where their street crossed Haight. Country Joe And The Fish had a place nearby. Haight St was a medieval fair of tie-die, homegrown weed, long hair, and Owsley Stanley's much sought after blotters of LSD. Teenage kids all over America were either on their way or dreaming about this neighbourhood. The music scene included The Grateful Dead and The Jefferson Airplane, of course, but also Big Brother and The Holding Company with Janis Joplin on vocals, Quicksilver Messenger Service and Moby Grape. By this point, San Francisco was pretty pleased with itself. Things were 'real' there, unlike say, in LA. LA was The Beach Boys, The Monkees, and Hollywood. It was fake and commercial where San Francisco was earthy and authentic.

This was ridiculous, of course. The biggest acts in San Francisco were signed to major labels and the whole Haight Ashbury thing had already been declared dead in a 'death of the hippie' symbolic funeral the previous year. But The Doors were regarded with suspicion and, according to Ray Manzarek, they felt some pressure to impress the audience at their first gig at the famous Fillmore that night.

A hundred other bands would have begun with 'Break On Through', already deemed to be the first single from the new album. But The Doors were not any of those bands. And Jim Morrison was no ordinary lead singer. Jim decided they would open with 'When The Music's Over'. Keeping in mind that this song was not on the album they were supposed to be promoting and is a long and dark jam, this was, to put it mildly, a brave move. But, according to Ray, it was the right one. The audience was floored by this 'plastic band from LA'.

Ray Manzarek seems to be very fond of this song, in particular the recording of it. It had been in their set for a long time and grown into the version that appears on the record. It's not hard to imagine it being something of a highlight. Ray gives several pages of his memoir over to the recording session in his memoir. To him, this song was a pinnacle for the band, the delivery of the promise made through the long nights at London Fog and the Whisky followed by the growing buzz around the first album. The recording session promised to be something special as they planned to do it live on the floor. They decided not to use the bass player but to play it as they had for the last year and a half. Everyone was primed, except Jim. He didn't turn up.

The band decided to go ahead and record the instruments anyway. Jim would just have to find his way around the song when, and if, he turned up. Remarkably, he did just that the next day. Listen to it again and imagine Jim making all of that happen with headphones on, alone in a vocal booth. Again, a bit like his hero Frank Sinatra, he had great timing. Even later, when alcohol was seriously inhibiting his performances, he seemed to possess some instinctive notion of when to come in early or when to hold back. I sometimes think that in the endless discussions of his 'shaman-like' identity, this quality is too often underplayed.

The song opens with a funky Booker T-style organ measure. Robby's guitar work is brilliant in this song. His immediately recognisable flamenco blues-rock lead playing, an important feature of the work to come, comes to the fore on this song. His improvised solo over 56 bars, according to the guitarist, is mysterious and compelling. John Densmore's drumming is another underrated aspect of this band and his vast vocabulary is on show here.

The lyrics are an intriguing mix of Jim's cut-up style. *The Scream Of The Butterfly* was the name of a film he had seen on a marquee somewhere, but in the song, it becomes something that he wants to hear before *The Big Sleep*, another film title. It contains some of his most memorable phrases, 'alive she cried,' 'feast of friends', 'Cancel my subscription to the resurrection.' Roughly speaking, the song seems to be about the need to embrace life in the face of impending death, but unlike its companion piece, 'The End', there is almost no narrative structure. He is improvising with language here. Phrases like those mentioned above are there as much for the sound as they are for meaning. The 'earth' becomes an increasingly important idea in Jim's writing, as we will see, and here he decries the damage we have done to it. The battle cry of 'We want the world and we want it Now' echoes the demonstration chant of 'what do we want? Peace! When do we want it? Now' and suggests that Jim was tuned in to the politics of the counterculture. This, too, would become a theme in his writing.

According to some sources, 'When The Music's Over' was their third most played song live, behind 'Light My Fire' and 'Back Door Man'. Certainly, there are versions on most of the live albums available. The *Live At The Hollywood Bowl 1968* version is a winner and there is excellent colour footage as a bonus.

Waiting For The Sun (1968)

Recorded: January to May 1968 at TTG Studios, Hollywood, California
Released: July 1968
Label: Elektra
Producer: Paul Rothchild
Engineer: Bruce Botnick
Additional musicians: Doug Lubahn (bass guitar), Kerry Magness (bass on 'The Unknown Soldier'), Leroy Vinnegar (stand up bass on 'Spanish Caravan')
Running Time: 33:10
Highest Chart Position: US: 1, UK: 16

Joan Didion is an American novelist, essayist, screenwriter, and memoirist. Her career stretches back to the late 1950s and she remains a keen observer of American culture. In 2017, a documentary called *Joan Didion: The Center Will Not Hold* was released. In it, she was interviewed about her time in Los Angeles in the late 1960s. She says that she was 'crazy about The Doors' and the interviewer asks why. With her hands moving animatedly around her face, she says simply: 'Bad boys'.

In 1968, while the band was recording *Waiting For The Sun*, Didion visited the studio and wrote about the experience in her 1979 book, *The White Album*. She lists everything that was in place there. The bass player, Doug Lubahn from Clear Light, Rothchild, Botnick, a dog called Nikki, food, and a 'couple of girls', along with Ray, John and Robby. Everything they needed, she writes, except Jim Morrison. Eventually, he turns up and sits on a couch, lighting matches. Nothing about Didion's account suggests any kind of real energy. She doesn't say much more, but the implication is a band bored with fame.

Waiting For The Sun was their only number one album released during their career. It wasn't well-reviewed, but it was, and remains a popular record. 'Hello I Love You' was a hit all over the world and made them even more famous than they already were in the wake of 'Light My Fire'. There are plenty of interesting moments and 'deep cuts' on this album, yet one can't help but feeling that something is missing. The first two albums are superb, where *Waiting For The Sun* is merely good, with some great tracks. They started work on it only a matter of months after *Strange Days* had been released. What had happened?

Jim Morrison did not cope well with fame. Ray Manzarek suggests that these sessions were the first indication that his drinking problem was going to be a serious problem for the band. And this is after being arrested onstage! John Densmore found the sessions excruciating and even quit at one point before being convinced by Robby to return. Morrison frequently didn't turn up or did so drunk. He brought unpleasant companions with him and turned in indifferent performances.

But it wasn't just Jim. Robby Kreiger has said, on several occasions, that the first two albums were comprised of songs that had been part of their set

45

at the Whisky. The lyrics were largely from Jim's 1965 notebooks. Now, they were running short of material. It's not an unusual problem for bands but most hit it on their second album, not their third. So we could consign any issues around this record to the 'difficult' follow up. Except that wouldn't be the whole story.

Paul Rothchild was a wonderful producer and responsible for many great albums by a wide range of artists in the 1960s. His sensitive work and keen instincts are some of the keys to Elektra's remarkable legacy. However, I will contend that he made a mess of this album and probably the next one as well. They still made some of the most exhilarating rock and roll of the era, but he made some serious tactical errors, and they had a lasting effect.

The Doors were intelligent guys who had, without anyone's help, already created an original rock and roll band that combined a theatrical stage presence with good music and seriously interesting lyrics. Their instincts were good. Jim knew somehow that his lyrics needed music and Ray heard it when Jim sang 'Moonlight Drive' on the beach. John Densmore was a sensitive and versatile drummer who added plenty of ideas to the mix. Robby Kreiger remains underrated as a guitar player and composer. My point is that they were perfectly capable of conceptualizing a direction for the band after their initial success.

The original idea for *Waiting For The Sun* was that one side would be given over to a long-form piece called 'The Celebration Of The Lizard'. It was a mix of spoken word and musical sections, including 'Not To Touch The Earth', which did appear on the record. It was recorded and, at least to my ears, is stunning. I will discuss it in more detail at the end of this section. The album would have been four or five songs on one side with 'The Celebration Of The Lizard' on the other. It would have allowed The Doors to continue to push the boundaries. Their 'cool' factor would have remained intact and the permission they had given themselves on tracks like 'Horse Latitudes' and 'The End' would have been fully realised.

But Paul Rothchild didn't like it. Or maybe he couldn't see the dollar signs. It seems clear to me that a decision was made to move the band in a pop direction. Jim was an appealing lead singer, and there was nothing to stop them from recording an album that would sell millions. He was right about creating an album that would sell but, in doing so, he second-guessed the band and I believe that they skipped a beat and missed what was a natural step forward.

Without 'The Celebration Of The Lizard', they had to scramble for material. Robby wrote three songs. They drew on the dregs of Jim's notebook and came up with a collection that could have been a lot better. Most books gloss over Rothchild's rejection of the cycle as though it makes perfect sense. I think it is a watershed moment. The band had lost their agency and it was a long time before they were able to recover it. By then, it was almost too late.

But, *Waiting For The Sun* is still a pretty good album.

Side One

'Hello, I Love You' (Morrison, Manzarek, Kreiger, Densmore)

This song was a very early one that appears on the World Pacific demo from 1965. It apparently came about when Jim observed a beautiful woman on Venice Beach. It has been described as the worst pickup line in rock and roll. The lyrics are not deep but fun in a sort of dated way.

This was part of Paul Rothchild's solution to the problem presented by taking out 'The Celebration Of The Lizard'. In a quest for material, Jac Holzman's son Adam remembered the song from the demo and suggested they revisit it. Rothchild, who admittedly had very good ears, knew a hit when he heard it. It was the second single released from the album and it charted all over the world. In the US. It battled it out for the number one spot with José Feliciano's version of 'Light My Fire'. It was one of the first stereo 45s.

Rothchild knew a hit, but perhaps not the ones by The Kinks. There is some disagreement about the extent to which anyone realised how close the chords were to 'All Day And All Of The Night'. Robby and John thought they were ripping off Cream's 'Sunshine of Your Love'! The demo does not sound like The Kink's song. Robby joined the band after the demos were made so perhaps it is his fault. Ray Davies was never much interested in suing anyone, but he wanted them to admit that there was a similarity. His lawyers felt differently, and a UK judge ordered that the appropriate share of the UK royalties be paid to Ray. The question is where Ray Davies found the progression. Very little is original in rock and roll.

The song damaged their reputation. Barney Hoskyns calls it 'sub bubblegum', and his view was more or less shared by the serious rock critics of the time, particularly the ones in San Francisco. The song's success and Jim's subsequent identity as a 'teen idol' seemed to give the critics and the counterculture the excuse they needed to dismiss The Doors. It didn't matter that The Grateful Dead were on a much more corporate label or that Jimi Hendrix had hit records; Jim Morrison was being held to different standards. This was not Mickey Dolenz. Jim Morrison was erudite and dangerous. It was already clear by 1968 that his revolutionary instincts were not drawn from the standard hippie playbook. He was a threat, not just to the establishment but the establishment within the anti-establishment. This record gave people like Jerry Garcia an excuse to point to him and say, 'see, he's a phoney'.

In any case, it remains one of their best-loved songs. Yes, it's pop, but so are 'White Rabbit' and 'Purple Haze'. It's memorable, danceable, and further proof that pop, poetry or revolution, Jim was indeed the lizard king and he could do anything.

'Love Street' (Morrison, Manzarek, Kreiger, Densmore)

This is one of The Doors' most sublime moments. It was the flipside to 'Hello I Love You' but probably could have held its own as an A-side. It's beautifully played, and Jim delivers the story well. The question of how personal

Morrison's lyrics were is a difficult one, but this song appears to be based on a particular moment in his life. It is often described as a song depicting his briefly idyllic time in Laurel Canyon with his girlfriend, Pamela Courson. That seems to be the case, but it is still a Doors song and is not without some darkness.

The story is that Jim and Pamela were living in Laurel Canyon in 1966 while the band was recording the first album. Laurel Canyon is a neighbourhood in Hollywood Hills. In the 1960s, despite being close to the action on the Sunset Strip, it seemed like another, more rustic world. Its place in rock and roll history is a big one. David Crosby, Stephen Stills, and Graham Nash found themselves harmonising together one night at Mama Cass's place there, for example. The parties were legendary, but the jam sessions that took place made it a laboratory for a whole range of musical styles, from folk rock, to country rock, to whatever Frank Zappa's brand of rock is called. 'Love Street' is far from the only song set there, either. 'Our House' by CSN was about the cottage where Graham Nash lived with Joni Mitchell. Joni gave her third album the elegant title, *Ladies of the Canyon*. Various Mamas and Papas lived there and inspired John Phillips' mildly creepy 'Twelve Thirty (Young Girls Are Coming To The Canyon)'. John Mayall recorded an album called *Blues From Laurel Canyon*. Jackie DeShannon's 'Laurel Canyon', also the title of the album, is a dreamy tribute to the place. This is an endless list. There are several books about Laurel Canyon in the '60s and '70s, but I would start with Barney Hoskyns' 2005 study, *Hotel California*.

The street in question is not called Love Street. The less whimsical Rothdell Trail runs behind the Canyon Store (where the creatures meet). Jim and Pamela named it Love Street as they watched the hippies wander around from their balcony. The house is still there, though it was damaged in a fire at some point and the balcony is gone. The Canyon Store is still thriving.

The lyrics do not present quite as idyllic a picture as one might think. 'I would like to see what happens' is not a particularly optimistic line. 'I guess I like it fine, so far' seems a bit fatalistic too. Something about her 'diamond-studded flunkeys' seems sinister. 'Our House', it ain't! There is an idea that The Doors ran out of material once they had exhausted Jim's famous 1965 notebook. It's clear that his demons prevented him from doing that sort of focussed work again, but a song like 'Love Street' is evidence that in 1966 he was still writing and, in my opinion, doing it very well. It is one of his most realised songs.

'Not To Touch The Earth' (Morrison, Manzarek, Kreiger, Densmore)

The best song on the album? Likely, and further evidence of a missed opportunity. This is a section of 'The Celebration Of The Lizard' cycle that was supposed to constitute the first side of *Waiting For The Sun*. It is a psychedelic masterpiece and certainly on the shortlist for the best Doors song most people have never heard. The title comes from a supplement to George Frazier's *The*

Golden Bough, a highly influential sourcebook for all things esoteric from
the turn of the last century. Part anthropology, part comparative religion,
part poppycock, it was a product of the fin de siècle fascination with the
occult, theosophical inquiry, and a romantic view of the 'other' in the colonial
landscape. Rituals, ceremonies, magic, shamans, fertility cults, and wounded
kings it's essentially a 600 page Doors song. It was also something that T.S.
Eliot found useful when he was writing, among other things, The Wasteland. It
was an influence on Yeats, Robert Graves, and significantly, Carl Jung. It had a
significant influence on modernism and the discipline of comparative religion.

It's not clear how much connection there is to the actual text. My hunch
is that he read the chapter headings: 'Not To Touch The Earth' (ch. 65) and
'Not To See The Sun' (ch. 66) and thought, 'I'll have those', before recording
them in his notebook. That said, the song is a Wasteland style nightmare. The
speaker uses the two lines to suggest, as usual, a mode of escape. 'Run with
me ... let's run' is another in a long series of songs about escape. The journey
stops first at a mysterious mansion where, rather clumsily, 'red are the chairs'.
There is then an abrupt shift to a 'dead president's corpse' in a car, seemingly
a reference to JFK's recent-ish assassination. Then we are in the old west with
'outlaws' and, in a classic Morrison image, a minister's daughter who is in love
with a snake in a well by the side of the road. The glancing reference both
to original sin and perhaps D.H. Lawrence's poem, 'The Snake', are worth
considering. The song ends with the possibility of reaching a destination with
the gates and the speaker's declaration of reptilian nobility.

Jim's nightmarish vision is perfectly accented by the musical accompaniment.
Everyone is at full throttle. John Densmore pounds out an insistent tattoo,
while Ray sounds like a demented church organist alongside Robby's fuzz box
twists. It is a magnificent sonic experience, particularly on headphones.

'Summer's Almost Gone' (Morrison, Manzarek, Kreiger, Densmore)

This is usually consigned to the filler box when this album is under discussion,
but it is, in fact, a gem, if not a full-blown 'deep cut'. It dates back to the
pre-Robby 1965 demo and presumably Jim's original notebook. The review
in *Rolling Stone* at the time thought the song was evocative despite the lame
lyrics. I don't agree. It is a simple song, but the repeated line 'morning found
us calmly unaware' is lovely and captures the lazy mood of summer. The
'laughing sea' is an appealing image and the question of where we'll be when
summer ends evokes the poetic idea of summer as youth.

The arrangement does not deviate wildly from that of the 1965 demo. In
tempo and atmosphere, it sounds like a psychedelic version of the Brian
Hyland 1962 hit 'Sealed With A Kiss'. Robby plays an eerie slide measure over
Ray's plaintive piano chords.

It's easy to dismiss this as one of the songs they dug up to fill the gap left by
Rothchild's rejection of The Celebration of the Lizard. While it may not be a

major statement, it is a trippy little sleeper that will grow on the listener with repeated listens.

'Wintertime Love' (Morrison, Manzarek, Kreiger, Densmore)

This is another one that is too often dismissed as filler on this record. It is a Robby Kreiger composition, so the lyrics are perhaps more predictably pop than the theatrical scripts in Morrison's ongoing psychodrama. They are light but evocative in their way. The waltz-time suits the band and Jim sings well. Ray's harpsichord solo over Doug Lubahn's lovely bass adds to the European feel of the song. It makes for a pleasant interlude at the end of side one before the onslaught of 'The Unknown Soldier'.

'The Unknown Soldier' (Morrison, Manzarek, Kreiger, Densmore)

I don't care for this song, I have to admit. Somewhere along the line, someone must have suggested an anti-war song, and this was the result. The Doors had been many things but never clumsy or bombastic. As a protest song, it protests too much and sounds a bit hollow. Musically, it's a solid Doors rocker with Ray out in front and Robby's always capable rhythm playing. John Densmore can relive his marching band days in the 'execution' section in the middle of the song. There is nothing wrong with Jim's performance. It is a theatrical song, and he delivers his lines with appropriate emotion.

The video, which was banned, is worth watching because it returns the lyrics to a more recognizable context. It opens with a series of streets scenes while Jim tells the story of the unknown soldier struck dead by a bullet in the head and how this plays out for the 'Television children' who hear about it over breakfast. The terms of this protest seem to take in everything from the cost of war in human terms to the consequences of mass media coverage of it. But then, in the video clip, Jim is tied up under the Santa Monica pier and executed. He looks like he has had a big night and when he spits up what I assume is supposed to be blood, it's hard to decide if he is dead or just hungover. The rest of the band play Indian instruments under the pier and then leave, accompanied by Nikki the husky. The rest of the clip is news footage from the Vietnam War.

It's easy to find this all a bit hilarious in retrospect, but, to be fair, all of the three younger members of the band had brushes with the draft board, and Ray got as far as Thailand when he was drafted in the early '60s. Early 1968 was the time of the TET Offensive and the escalation of the war was an issue as prescient as anything you can think of today. The song works better live. The clip of the Hollywood Bowl performance and Jim's impressive stage fall, after the shot rings out, gives the song the theatrical context it requires.

There is some subtext for Jim Morrison, as he had grown up in a military family. His father was a decorated war hero who had served in Korea and had recently been promoted to the lofty rank of Rear admiral in the Navy. There is no evidence that his father ever pressured him to serve in the military – just imagine that for a second – or that they clashed on the subject of the war. But the video does suggest that the song runs deeper than it might seem for Jim Morrison.

It is worth pointing out that the sound of the cocked rifles in the song is courtesy of the rock critics Paul Williams and Richard Goldstein, who were on hand to serve in the studio and do their duty for the band. Kerry Magness, who was in The Kingsmen and an early incarnation of Rhinoceros, plays bass on this one.

This was probably the first song recorded for the album and it was the first single. It squeezed into the *Billboard* Top Forty but was deemed too controversial by many stations.

Side Two
'Spanish Caravan' (Morrison, Manzarek, Kreiger, Densmore)
The second side opens with a gloriously romantic song written by Robby Kreiger and features yet another facet of his considerable skill as a guitar player. It is truly a high point on this album, and it is a bit difficult to understand why it doesn't seem to ever been considered for release as a single. Sure, the lyrics are a bit daft. Why would a Spanish galleon be found lost in the trade winds? Unlike the light breezes of the horse latitudes, the trade winds were reliable for sailing. I'm a bit surprised that the Admiral's son, Jim, didn't mention this to Robby.

But the arrangement is thrilling. It begins with Robby first playing something like a flamenco study known as a Granadias for the first 30 seconds or so before moving into a section of 'Asturias' by Issac Albeniz. The band was sued by a small French publishing company for the Granadias section. As one might imagine, the intro to the song is widely discussed online and there are many opinions on exactly what is being referenced by Robby here. What is interesting to me is the mix of classical and flamenco styles in a short introduction.

The first half of the song is just Jim and Robby with occasional cymbal sounds from John Densmore. Robby was apparently playing a Ramirez classical guitar. At a certain point, the song stops completely before we hear a fuzzy electric guitar playing the Albeniz piece. Ray's trademark swirling organ comes in to create an Iberian psychedelic dreamscape. It's particularly thrilling on headphones.

There are at least two filmed live versions online, which are well worth watching. Jim does his unique one maraca shake at the beginning of the Hollywood Bowl 1968 version. The song appears here and there on their setlists until early 1969, sometimes as part of a medley. It hasn't been covered all that often, but a version by Hobo Blues Band in Hungarian is worth hearing.

'My Wild Love' (Morrison, Manzarek, Kreiger, Densmore)
This does not sound like any other Doors song. It is sung in the manner of a work song and the instrumentation is limited to handclaps, a rattle, and

perhaps a few drum beats here and there. The lyrics tell yet another story of a journey that is at once an actual journey and a spiritual one seeking freedom. The narrator's love rides from place to place – a farm, Christmas, Japan – taking the occasional rest but then moving on. It's a Western; it's a fantastical quest; it's a Doors song.

The idea may have come from Robby, who admired, as we have noted, Koerner, Ray, and Glover, a blues trio whose first album begins with a work song, 'Linin Track'. The form goes back at least to the 19th century, and work songs were among those collected by the first generation of scholars making field recordings in the American south. The folksinger, Odetta, is not as well-remembered as she should be these days, but one of her signature songs was 'Waterboy', a work song of sorts. She often performed acapella material on stage like 'God's Gonna Cut You Down'. It's not hard to hear something of Odetta's influence on 'My Wild Love'.

'We Could Be So Good Together' (Morrison, Manzarek, Kreiger, Densmore)

Even The Doors have off days. This track was recorded for one of the first two albums and rejected. It's not entirely clear if this is a re-recording or, as they say, something prepared earlier. It could have been on any The Doors album thus far and my guess is that it was recorded for the first album. Again, the rejection of 'The Celebration Of The Lizard' meant that second rate songs made it onto an album in the absence of stronger new material. There is nothing wrong with this song; it's just very light. The lyrics don't break any new ground, but they do again reveal Jim's inability to write a straight love song. It all sounds promising at the beginning of the song, but by the end, angels are being beheaded. The band chugs along for the ride in a merry if unexceptional manner. Ray is doing his best Alan Price imitation when he isn't quoting Thelonious Monk just after Robby's guitar solo. It was the flipside to 'The Unknown Soldier' but never seems to have been a feature of their live shows. It's not filler because The Doors couldn't do filler if they tried, but it is perhaps slight compared to most of the other material on this record.

'Yes, The River Knows' (Morrison, Manzarek, Kreiger, Densmore)

This is one of those Doors songs that would have all but their most invested fans scratching their heads. It was written by Robby and is a small gem rarely mentioned in reviews or articles about this record. Online, the discussion generally focuses on whether Jim is saying 'mysticated wine' or 'mystic heated wine'. One thing for sure, it isn't 'masticated wine' as it appears on a never reliable lyrics website.

Robby once again proves to be the folk/world influence in the band, with a song that sounds like it could be a lost Child Ballad as rendered by Nick Drake, with what sounds like a reference to Clarence's sad fate in Shakespeare's

Richard III. Robby's lyrics are usually compared unfavourably with Jim's, and it is clear that he did not have the literary chops. But this song shows his skills developing. The river works well as a metaphor for passing time in a bittersweet song about drifting apart from someone.

Jim sings this very well. His plaintive delivery of 'please believe me' at the beginning is a good example of the drama he could introduce in a song when he wasn't bored or drunk or both. Ray's lyrical piano line follows the vocal closely. Paul Rothchild, whose ambitions as a George Martin style producer were becoming a problem for the band, demonstrates how good he is with an understated arrangement here.

With Jim's increasingly erratic behaviour and a shortage of material, this song represents a promising direction both in production and style. Unfortunately, they didn't take it, and quiet songs like this were buried under horn sections on their next album.

'Five To One' (Morrison, Manzarek, Kreiger, Densmore)

Yes, this was the song that the band was doing that night in 1969 at the Dinner Key Theatre in Miami when Jim unleashed his inner crawling kingsnake from its leather panted prison. If that's what he did. The other Doors have all given wildly inconsistent accounts and the crowd saw what they wanted to see. The police knew what they had seen. The band was behind him after all and presumably, the police were watching the crowd to make sure everyone was having good decent fun. There is no footage, but there is a recording and Jim does seem to be in a particularly aggressive state. Not that the crowd notices. Came for the songs, stayed for the riot. Only Jim could get a cheer calling his audience 'fucking idiots' and suggesting that maybe they love being pushed around. He then tells them they are a bunch of slaves. He sounds insane. The fact is that he was drunk that night in Miami, and it is not a great performance of this song. If you have ever been berated by a hard drinker in a pub, you will recognise what is going on here.

But his blood alcohol level shouldn't have made a difference because, according to Densmore and Manzarek, he was drunk when he recorded it in the first place. And not just tipsy. He needed to be held up while he belted out the lyrics. It's not his greatest vocal performance, but it's hard to believe that someone that drunk could still sing at all.

By this point, the last song on the album spot was reserved for a BIG song like 'The End', or 'When The Music's Over'. I don't think this one stands up to either, but it still compelling in its way. In his memoir, John Densmore says that he asked Jim about the ratio in the title. 'That's for me to know', said Jim stumbling off to the toilet. There are a lot of theories. The baby boom was big enough that at the time, someone was predicting that young people would soon outnumber old people by five to one. Some people think it might have been a reference to the number of African American to white soldiers serving in Vietnam. Others think it is a reference to the rather dire odds in Russian roulette. My theory is this: the line that follows, 'no one gets out of here alive', is one of the few certainties of this life, along with taxes. 'Five to one / One in five', the odds don't matter because death is a certainty. It's not a very uplifting theory, but there you are.

Related Songs
'The Celebration Of The Lizard' (Morrison, Manzarek, Kreiger, Densmore)

I find this piece thrilling. Jim's shriek of 'Wake up!' after stating that the ceremony is about to begin never fails to send chills down my spine. It is rock and roll theatre and Jim's genius as an actor and performance artist is on full display here.

This spoken word and musical poem was, as I have suggested, a missed opportunity for the band. There was considerable work done on it in the studio and the recording made during the sessions for this album is, or would have been, one of The Doors' finest moments. It contains some of Jim's most representative and fully realised work. The Beat influence is obvious, but there are also traces of T. S. Eliot's 'The Wasteland', W.B. Yeats' 'The Second Coming', Arthur Rimbaud's 'A Season In Hell', and Shelley's famous nightmare of women with eyes instead of nipples. The thrilling opening lines, 'Lions in the street and roaming / Dogs in heat, rabid, foaming / A beast caged in the heart of a city' set the scene for another of Jim's great journeys through a fantastical but clearly American landscape. Instead of the rather trite 'I can do anything' line that finishes the abridgement 'Not To Touch The Earth', which appeared on the album, he finishes with the far more intriguing:

I am the Lizard King
Retire now to your tents and to your dreams
Tomorrow we enter the town of my birth
I want to be ready

Jim's vision reveals the depth of his literary imagination, but also his alertness to the countercultural rate of change and perhaps the darkness implicit in an age of uncertainty. Like the modernists he knew so well, there is the sense of something ominous on the horizon. Many writers have suggested that Morrison, almost alone, seemed to intuit the rise of the sort of forces that would so soon reveal the possibility of evil in the hippie dream of freedom.

Meanwhile, the rest of the band provides a cinematic soundtrack that has all the best elements of their music. Ray's eclectic organ veers from avant-garde jazz to Chicago blues while Robby improvises his parts in typical style. Anyone who doesn't rate John Densmore's percussion skills should listen closely to this on headphones. He is so creative and instinctive that it is impossible to think of another drummer of the period who would have been able to do what he does here.

Unfortunately, Paul Rothchild just couldn't see it. In an alternative universe, this was side one of 'Waiting For The Sun' and The Doors retained their underground credibility as leaders in innovative rock and roll. Morrison's considerable skills as a poet were taken seriously and he was invited to do readings instead of photoshoots for Tiger Beat. The band continued to record music but balanced it with spoken word pieces. Jim eventually left music for a distinguished career as a writer and won the Nobel the year he turned 75.

That's not what happened.

The Soft Parade (1969)

Recorded: March 1968 – June 1969 at Elektra Sound West, Hollywood, California
Released: July 1969
Label: Elektra
Producer: Paul Rothchild
Engineer: Bruce Botnick
Additional musicians: Doug Lubahn (bass guitar), Harvey Brooks (bass guitar),
Curtis Amy (saxophone), Jesse McReynolds (mandolin), Jim Buchanan (fiddle)
Running Time: 33:50
Highest Chart Position: US: 6 UK: Did not chart

The Soft Parade is widely considered to be the band's worst album. Jim
Morrison thought it lacked a narrative. Robby Kreiger thinks The Doors' sound
was buried by Paul Rothchild's heavy-handed use of strings and horns. *Rolling
Stone* magazine said at the time that 'it is worse than infuriating, it's just sad'.
For other critics and the counterculture, it confirmed that The Doors were
finished as a serious rock and roll band. It landed in the middle of an annus
horribilis for the group, which saw the band almost unable to play live after
the famous Miami incident. If 1968 had been the beginning of Jim Morrison's
struggles with fame and alcohol, 1969 was when he seemed to descend into
madness. The recording of the Miami show is excruciating but also oddly
compelling. Sure, one could write Morrison off as a nasty drunk with a
microphone, but somewhere in there is something akin to the postmodern
theatrical experiments that took place throughout the 20th century. Provocative
doesn't quite capture it. Before the alleged public revelation of 'The Lizard', he
is calling the audience 'fucking idiots' and 'slaves'. It's theatre, but the fourth
wall is truly breached. I doubt many punks in 1977 gave much thought to Jim
Morrison, but it really had all been done before.

Unfortunately, *The Soft Parade* does not, in any sense, illuminate Jim's
revolutionary program, if there was one, or capture any interesting bits of his
state of mind. Of course, that would have been very difficult at the time. Part
of the problem here, and it is something that was becoming more obvious on
Waiting For The Sun, is Jim's absence. He turns up to sing, but if the first two
albums reflected his artistic ideas, this album belongs to others in the band and
on the production team. Rothchild said, at some stage, that 'as the talent fades,
the producer has to become more active.' This was emerging on *Waiting For
The Sun* but is beyond doubt on *The Soft Parade*.

It's easy to point to Paul Rothchild for the unevenness of *The Soft Parade*,
but that may be unfair. I sense that he is more to blame for *Waiting For
The Sun*'s shortcomings than for most of those on this album. He was in
the unenviable position of making an album with Elektra's most lucrative
band while under some pressure as a producer to get the car out of the
psychedelic garage. It turns out, too, that Ray Manzarek was also interested
in expanding The Doors' sound. Popular music was moving very quickly in

the late '60s. Their first album was recorded in 1966 under the spell of Them, The Seeds, The Animals and the early San Francisco psychedelic bands. By 1969, Blood Sweat and Tears had released their self-titled and enormously popular second album. It is one of the starting points for the rather vague genre of 'jazz rock' and was very influential at the time. For Manzarek, a serious jazz fan, and the eclectic Robby Kreiger, it must have seemed like a very appealing direction. Indeed, Ray Manzarek, in his memoir, calls *The Soft Parade* 'one of our most innovative albums' and has only good memories of its creation.

It's worth listening to the Blood Sweat and Tears album for some context. *The Soft Parade* does not sound much like the first three Doors albums or the two that followed it. It is, as some have suggested, something of a failed experiment, though comparisons to affable train wrecks like The Rolling Stones' *Their Satanic Majesties Request* are unfair. It is more like an interesting misstep, a challenging and somewhat perplexing record that will grow with some persistence. Approached with fresh ears, it might even become a favourite.

Side One
'Tell All The People' (Kreiger)
By the time *The Soft Parade* appeared, a lot of the material had already appeared on singles. 'Tell All The People', the third one, was released in June of 1969. It took a couple of months to reach its peak at 57 on the *Billboard* charts. Jim Morrison was on trial in Miami and the band wasn't touring. Radio stations were no longer much interested in The Doors and their credibility had hit rock bottom by this point.

It was written by Robby Kreiger, and Jim Morrison was not keen on it. He said it was dumb and particularly objected to the line, 'Can't you see me growing, get your guns'. He objected to this song so stridently that he insisted that the writing credits would henceforth reflect the actual writers of the song rather than just The Doors, as it had been on the first three albums. He really didn't like this song.

In 2019, a deluxe 50th-anniversary edition of *The Soft Parade* featured Robby Kreiger's new mixes of each song without the horns. Whatever one thinks about 'Tell All The People', it is pretty clear that Paul Rothchild's original idea for the arrangement was spot on. The drama is greatly enhanced by the horns, and the glorious sweep of 'Tell all the people that you see / Follow me' needs fanfare. Jim may not have loved singing it, but his performance is solid. It was one of the first songs recorded for the album and the singer is in full crooner mode until he takes it up to a bluesy growl late in the song. Critics have suggested that he sounds bored, but I don't agree. He doesn't sound overly interested in the story, as it is, but he finds the right tone.

Despite the elaborate arrangement, the band played it live as late as 1970. There is a version online from a television show called *Critique*.

'Touch Me' (Kreiger)

This was The Doors' final visit to the top ten in the US during their career. It was the first single from *The Soft Parade* and appeared in December 1968, more than six months before the release of the album. It's sobering to think that 'Light My Fire', their first top ten single, had only been about 18 months earlier. The pace of the development of rock and roll in the late sixties is astonishing and no more so than with this band.

The original title of this Kreiger song was 'Hit Me', but according to some sources, Morrison wasn't prepared to sing 'c'mon, c'mon and hit me' to his increasingly fractious audiences. Considering that he regularly berated them for their apathy and seemed to enjoy whipping them up into some sort of Dionysian fury, it's a bit hard to believe that he was worried about this title. Maybe he just thought 'Touch Me' was more effective. He was right. Kreiger supposedly wrote it as a declaration of love. The 'I'm going to love you until the heaven stops the rain' etc. sentiment is pretty standard, but the curious questions, 'What was that promise that you made? / Won't you tell me what she said?' suggest a more complicated story. Who is this other 'she'? And what did she say?

I'm not sure why this wasn't the first track on the album, but then there are any number of questions one could raise about the songs that were chosen, the track order, and everything else about *The Soft Parade*. The opening section sets up a thrilling stop where Jim sings 'cmon, cmon' before the band kicks in again. Jim delivers the song with great style and attack. It is on songs like this one where his gift as a rock and roll crooner is most obvious. He doesn't growl; he doesn't turn into Bob Dylan or Mick Jagger and sing it all from the roof of his mouth. Like David Clayton-Thomas, he opens his throat and draws the sound up from his belly. It's remarkable when one considers that he had been singing professionally for less than three years. Just about everyone involved with this record has suggested that Jim was bottoming out with alcohol at the time. I'm sure this is true, but he was still able to turn in some remarkable performances, and this is one of them.

The band, expanded considerably with Harvey Brooks on bass, a horn section, and strings, still sounds like The Doors. Again, Robby Kreiger's Doors only mix is interesting but lacks the drama of the original. Something about the horns answering Jim in the chorus gives the song a real punch. The string section around the 'I'm going to love you' section is too lush for this band but isn't the total catastrophe that critics of the time thought it was. Before you read any further, you should stop and watch the clip of The Doors playing this song on the *Smothers Brothers* television show. Jim amid risers supporting the string and horn sections wouldn't have done much for their credibility, but it's a terrific clip. Robby Kreiger has a black eye, the real sort as opposed to the kind you see in movies, and Jim appears to be in reasonably good form.

The sax player in the clip is Curtis Amy, who plays the solo at the end of the recording. Amy was a veteran of Ray Charles' band and would later play

on Carole King's *Tapestry* album. The sax solo, once a staple of rock and roll
songs, had given way to the electric guitar by 1968 and was still more than
a decade away from the resurgence in the '80s. Amy's works very well here.
The various live versions that he played on, notably the one on the *Live At The
Aquarius* album, show that it is one of the song's key elements. Jim Morrison
said that he was proud of it because it was the first 'jazz' solo in a rock and roll
song. Even a quick sampling of Lee Allen's work in the 1950s would suggest
that isn't the case, but we sort of know what he means. It is a departure from
the sax solos on Motown songs and surf instrumentals and it does drift into
something like hard bop towards the end. For trivia night, Curtis Amy was
married to Merry Clayton, whose vocals are so striking on the Rolling Stones'
'Gimme Shelter'.

Like 'Tell All The People', this turned up live now and again in 1969, but only
once or twice after the tour for this album. There are no particularly notable
covers of the song though it was recorded by several bands, including the
usual suspects, The Lettermen, after its release. Robby Kreiger, at some point,
came clean and acknowledged the obvious source of The Four Seasons' 'Cmon
Marianne'. Listen for yourself.

'Shaman's Blues' (Morrison)

More than a few people have commented on this song sounding more like The
Doors than anything else on *The Soft Parade*. It is something of the throwback
to their more garage days, and it isn't hard to imagine it on their first album.
No offence to Robby, but it is something of a relief after the first two songs to
hear Jim singing his own words again. The title sounds like a throwaway and
doesn't capture the theme of loneliness and despair. There is some idea that
Pamela Courson, the probable subject of several of Jim's songs, had taken
off to Europe with someone else. The surreal landscape of this song includes
meadows, train yards, a penitentiary, and 'Saturday's shore'. 'Your moves and
your mind' is possibly a reference to Ezra Pound's opening line in 'Portrait
d'un Femme', 'You and your mind are our Sargasso Sea'.

The song begins with the crash of Ray's harpsichord before the central bass
riff kicks in. Robby's lead guitar hovers over Ray's organ. Ray takes the first
solo, followed by Robby. The song ends with Jim chatting over the music,
apparently spliced together from various takes.

This is a cool song and one of the highlights of the album. It doesn't seem to
have featured in their live set, which is odd because it's an upbeat, riff-y song
that would have worked well on stage.

'Do it' (Morrison, Kreiger)

Ray Manzarek calls this one a 'jazz-inspired rocker'. It begins with what sounds
like a splice of someone, maybe Ray, counting in the band before Jim's hearty
laugh kicks the song off for real. It is more of a riff than a song, but it's a good
riff. The lyrics, apparently a collaboration between Robby and Jim, say exactly

nothing beyond 'Please, please, listen to me children' with sundry other lines here and there. Is it a cult leader's refrain or a schoolteacher's plea? Who knows, but it sounds great in Jim's deep tones. I'm not sure where the jazz comes in, but it rocks along with a neat little riff answering Jim. The middle eight section with its driving bass sounds promising but doesn't go anywhere too revealing. It attracted the ire of more than a few reviewers for the paucity of lyrics. It's something of a grower on this strange album, but it does seem unfinished. That's a shame because it could have been a great song. This one doesn't seem to have ever made it into their live set, either.

'Easy Ride' (Morrison)

This was a song recorded for *Waiting For The Sun* and the recording here predates the rest of the material on this album. It was part of their live set as early as 1967, so it might have represented a 'go to' when they were scrambling for material on *Waiting For The Sun,* and indeed on *The Soft Parade*. Ray Manzarek calls it a 'country rocker by way of Muddy Water's Got My Mojo Working', which is pretty accurate. It's not a particularly interesting song musically, though it does show, I believe, the influence of CCR, the ranking American band of the time. Jim's lyrics, possibly cobbled together from bits and pieces in his original notebooks, are much darker than the light arrangement might suggest. 'The mask that you wore / My fingers would explore / Costume of control / Excitement soon unfolds', is firmly in Velvet Underground territory with what would appear to be a reference to bondage gear. 'Ride' or 'rider' was a popular double entendre in early blues, and the phrase 'easy rider' had a long history before it was associated with the 1969 film.

Side Two
'Wild Child' (Morrison)

A highlight of this record, 'Wild Child' is another song that could have appeared on the first or second album. It is built around the sort of appealing blues riff that would become a staple of hard rock in the years to come. It was the B-side of 'Touch Me' and the other song that they performed on the *Smothers Brothers* TV show in December of 1968.

The lyrics are Jim's, and they are fascinating. On the one hand, he seems to be talking about a Christ figure. The 'wild child' is 'the saviour of the human race' and is not his parent's child. In the third verse, he shifts to another character, a temple dancer who is staring into the eyes of a hollow idol with her pirate prince at her side. The song ends with a question: 'Remember when we were in Africa?' So it seems to be a mix of the synoptic gospels, the Mahabharata, Gilbert and Sullivan, and the poet Arthur Rimbaud's escape to Africa. Ray Manzarek says it is about Danny Sugerman, who later co-wrote the famous biography of Morrison, *No One Here Gets Out Alive*, but in 1968 he was fourteen and working for The Doors answering their fan mail. Manzarek also suggests the song might be autobiographical.

There is a clip online of The Doors recording it in the studio. It's interesting to watch the process. Jim seems slightly spaced out but comes in at exactly the right time and performs the song with great depth and care. It's interesting to see both Paul Rothchild and Bruce Botnick hovering around Jim before the take. Robby opens with the lick using a slide before the rest of the band comes in. *The Soft Parade* is an album going in several directions at once, but this song points forward to the band's future embrace of a rawer blues sound.

'Runnin' Blue' (Kreiger)

Ray Manzarek calls it 'jazzy atonal country and western'. Richie Unterberger called it a 'strange bluegrass soul blend'. There is no question that 'Runnin' Blue' is one of the oddest songs in The Doors catalogue, which makes the fact that it was released as a single all the more curious. Like all of the singles released from this album, it was a Robby Kreiger composition. The story is that The Doors were scheduled to play a show with Otis Redding just after Christmas in 1967 at Winterland in San Francisco. Otis died in a plane crash on December 10th of that year and Robby was inspired to write the song. It was not a big hit and was not loved by the critics of the time. I will cautiously suggest that it has aged rather well and the stylistic juxtapositions in the age of sampling don't sound as jarring as they might have when the single appeared in 1969.

This is almost the only Doors release, in Morrison's lifetime, with a lead vocal from anyone else. Robby's slightly corny delivery of the chorus is just one element in an arrangement that includes mandolin work from bluegrass legend Jesse McReynolds (of Jim and Jesse), Jim Buchanan on fiddle, and a jazzy horn section. Robby puts in some solid work on lead guitar here as well. Jim Morrison's phrasing is particularly good in this song as he invests great drama into some fairly thin lyrics. The 'runnin'' blues seem to be a variation on the better known 'walkin'' blues, but what this has to do with Otis Redding is anyone's guess. It's also not clear why he thought he might find Otis' dock 'back in LA' when Otis' famous song is so clearly set in San Francisco.

This song divides Doors fans. It shouldn't work but still does somehow. The sheer originality of the arrangement, along with Robby's sincere grief for Otis, makes this a memorable track on *The Soft Parade*. As one might conclude, they didn't attempt it live, though the 'Poor Otis' section appears, seemingly improvised by Jim, at about the twelve-minute mark of 'When The Music's Over' at the 1967 Winterland gig where they were to appear with Redding. It turns up again in Chicago in May 1968 at the end of 'Soul Kitchen'.

'Wishful Sinful' (Kreiger)

This song is sometimes noted as the ultimate Doors 'deep cut', but it was in fact the second single released from *The Soft Parade* sessions and appears on various compilations. It is, like the other singles released from this album, a Robby Kreiger composition, and it appeared in March of 1969, several months before the actual LP turned up in July.

Ray Manzarek, always good for identifying the genre of Doors songs, says that Wishful Sinful is 'classical'. It's certainly a lush production with loping strings and brass but 'rock ballad' is probably closer to the mark. Robby Kreiger's stripped-back version is worth hearing to decide how you feel about the decorative elements provided by Paul Rothchild. I prefer the simpler version in this case. Jim does a good job of telling Robby's story here and the arrangements are distracting. Others may disagree.

It is essentially a love song, though there is something darker in the reference to water, especially when it 'covers you' in the last verse. It's important to remember that these were people who lived near the sea and probably swam often, so the usual ominous water imagery may not always apply.

A PBS television special entitled 'A Profile of Jim Morrison and The Doors – On and Off Stage' featured them performing the song in a studio, but it doesn't seem to have featured in their live shows at any point. Intriguingly, sixties rock classicists The Smithereens covered it a few times, but recordings are not easy to find.

'The Soft Parade' (Morrison)
Is there anything in rock and roll that even remotely resembles the first 35 seconds or so of this song? It's so utterly unexpected and strange that it never fails to make an impression, even after years of listening to this record. Suddenly, Jim is a preacher who recalls a discussion in seminary school about whether or not the lord can be petitioned with prayer. After repeating the question 'petition the lord with prayer?' twice, he explodes with the answer, 'you cannot petition the lord with prayer!' It is possible to listen to repeated takes of this sequence with Jim's voice growing huskier each time. There has always been talk of Jim as a 'shaman', but his ability as an actor is sometimes underplayed. This, like 'Horse Latitudes', and much of his spoken word work attests to his ability to bring language to life in the manner of a stage actor.

The title track is the fourth in a series of ambitious final album tracks for the band. It is more of a cycle than a song. The seminary sequence is followed by a plea for sanctuary, a lovely fragment that is far too short. This is followed by, to my ears anyway, perhaps the worst thing the band ever recorded. It sounds like the theme song to a long-forgotten sitcom with daft lyrics and a dreadful arrangement. This gives way to something almost as cloying that sounds like a grim parody of 'My Favourite Things'.

Fortunately, this is quickly replaced by the 'Soft Parade' section, which is more representative. This part could have easily stood alone, and with some work, might have been a genuine Doors classic. Unfortunately, it's part of an awkward medley with no overarching theme. The lyrics in this section evoke the counterculture as seen perhaps by Jim Morrison. It is decadent, exotic, and dangerous. Morrison uses, not for the first or last time, animal imagery. Cobras, leopards, a deer woman and 'the lions of the night' all make an appearance. At the end of the song, he invites someone to meet him at the edge of town, suggesting in a film noirish way that they 'better bring a gun'. In the final lines, he says that 'When all else fails / We can always whip the horses' eyes / And make them sleep / And cry....' It's a horrifying image, but it seems to belong to the night world dreamscape of the song.

It's difficult to know whether there was ever a concept for the cycle, or it was just Paul Rothchild cobbling together some fragments in an attempt to create something bigger than the sum of its parts. It remains an engaging listen, and the sly bossa nova boogie of the 'Soft Parade' section remains one of their great moments. It doesn't have the psychological menace of 'The End' or the gravity of 'When The Music's Over', but it seems like a fitting end to this rather odd album.

Related Tracks
'Who Scared You?' (Morrison, Kreiger)
This really might be the great Doors 'deep cut'. It was the flipside of 'Wishful Sinful', and it is easy to imagine that many fans preferred it to the A-side. Featuring a classic Kreiger solo and some light horns, it's arguably better than most of the songs on the actual album. It has a great riff and might have suited the album better than, say, 'Easy Ride'. It was recorded at about the same time as 'Shaman's Blues' in late 1968, so it isn't entirely clear why it was left off the record. Doors fans (like me, for instance) who came to this band a bit later via the *Weird Scenes Inside the Goldmine* compilation will remember this as a highlight.

'I Am Troubled' (Morrison)
A gentle little fragment of a song employing some of Jim's poetry.

'Rock Is Dead' (Morrison et al.)
This is the sort of thing that will test your admiration for this band. If you are a paid-up 'Doorshead', you will adore this hour-long freeform jam. If you are just a big fan, you might find it interesting to hear Jim's interpretation of some classic rock and roll songs and his reflections on the state of the genre. Morrison is in great voice, and the band seems to be having fun mixing things up and trading ideas. This session took place in early 1969, but it isn't hard to discern the direction they will take after *The Soft Parade*. To my ears, they are falling back on their sets at London Fog and the Whisky, where, until they became a 'thing', they were providing music for dancing and good times. It was bands like The Doors and Love that supplanted Johnny Rivers and Bill Lee Riley as residents on the Whisky Stage. Billy Lee Riley's live album recorded at the Whisky not long before The Doors turned up is a good indicator of what was demanded of bands on the Sunset Strip. He rips through a series of RnB standards with only enough variation to keep things interesting. In 'Rock is Dead', The Doors do something similar. There is a harrowing take on a Robert

Johnson style blues and some Morrison improvised poetry, but mainly they keep the groove going.

It's a gruelling listen at points, but in some ways, it is in such contrast to the high production values of *The Soft Parade,* that it is almost like the next Doors album in an alternative universe. It might test your patience, but it is certainly worth hearing once. There are edited versions here and there if you aren't prepared to take the full plunge. It's not entirely clear why it was recorded and doesn't seem to have ever been considered as part of *The Soft Parade* project. The story is that they went out for dinner after a long day of recording and came back and recorded it.

'Whiskey Mystics And Men' (Morrison)

This is one of those mysterious Doors tracks that were recorded but left unfinished and were never revisited. And that's a shame because it's a great song with a memorable beat and interesting lyrics. It's not clear exactly when it was recorded or if it was ever a serious contender for the album. It can be found on the 1997 *Perception* box set.

'Chaos' (The Doors)

Instrumental jam that finishes with Jim improvising around Little Willie John's 'Fever'. Not sure how this constitutes a song, but it is the final track on the 50th-anniversary edition of *The Soft Parade.*

Right: The cover for *London Fog.* It was The Doors' Hamburg. (*Rhino*)

Below: The Doors. The bar is half full of prostitutes, out of work actors, runaways, scene makers, junkies, students, and barflies. You look around and think, these people have found their band.

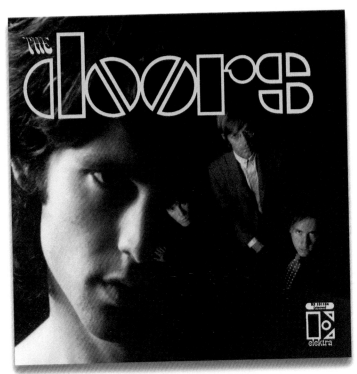

Left: A thrilling record and one of the great debuts in rock and roll history. (*Rhino*)

Right: Rock and roll is littered with one-hit wonders and disappointing second albums. *Strange Days* isn't one of them. (*Rhino*)

Above: By the time Jim got to his mother's room, the Whisky, filled with people wasted on a wide variety of substances, had gone very, very, quiet. (*Tony Thompson*)

Below: The street in question is not called Love Street. The less whimsical Rothdell Trail runs behind the Canyon Store (where the creatures meet). (*Tony Thompson*)

Above: 'Moonlight Drive' was, according to Manzarek, the song that Jim Morrison sang to him on the beach at Venice in the summer of 1965. (*Tony Thompson*)

Below: Ray thought Jim had moved to New York and was surprised to see his friend wandering, shirtless and starry-eyed, down the beach. Venice Beach boardwalk in 2019. (*Tony Thompson*)

Above: The Doors were scruffy beatniks from Venice. Venice Beach again, photographed by the author in 2019. (*Tony Thompson*)

Below: 'Hello I Love You' apparently came about when Jim observed a beautiful woman on Venice Beach. Venice Beach, California today. (*Tony Thompson*)

Left: The Doors' third album, *Waiting for The Sun*, released in 1968. (*Rhino*)

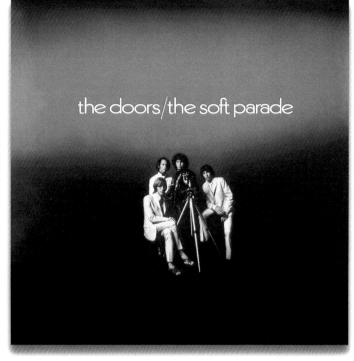

Right: It is more like an interesting misstep, a challenging and somewhat perplexing record that will grow with some persistence. *The Soft Parade*. (*Rhino*)

Left: Venice boardwalk, taken by the author in 2019. (*Tony Thompson*)

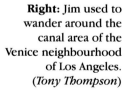

Right: Jim used to wander around the canal area of the Venice neighbourhood of Los Angeles. (*Tony Thompson*)

Left: The keyboard player is firing off little riffs on a Vox organ but is also covering the bass parts on a Fender Rhodes. Ray Manzarek executes the timeless organ intro to 'Light My Fire'.

Right: John Densmore's drumming is an underrated aspect of this band, and his vast vocabulary is on show.

Left: The Doors are on fire here, particularly Robby, whose guitar solo is astonishing.

Right: Jim was taking rock and roll in a direction suggested by the Beat poets a decade earlier.

Left: Ray provides eerie colour on the organ. Playing 'Love Me Two Times' on television.

Right: Jim said once that he was 'exploring the bounds of reality'. In their shows, he was exploring the bounds of the rock and roll live event, and he certainly pushed those boundaries.

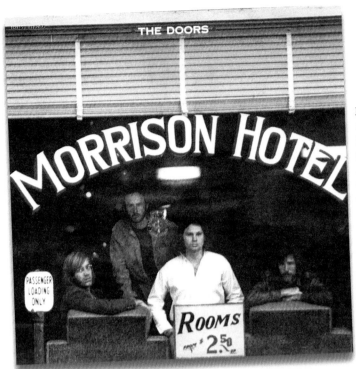

Left: Legendary rock photographer Henry Diltz did the cover shoot at Morrison Hotel very quickly after the day guy at the desk refused to allow the band to set up for a photoshoot. (*Rhino*)

Right: *Absolutely Live*. A Doors show was a spectacle, a mass meeting, and a gathering of the tribes. (*Rhino*)

Right: 'Into this world we're thrown...' Jim in the promo film for 'LA Woman'.

Left: The Doors playing 'Touch Me' on the Smothers Brothers television show. Robby has a black eye...

Right: Morrison, for his part, invents a sort of crooner rock and roll style that has been imitated endlessly ever since. Performing 'Touch Me' on US TV in 1968.

Left: Ray Manzarek said that *LA Woman* just 'fucking exploded' in the studio. (*Rhino*)

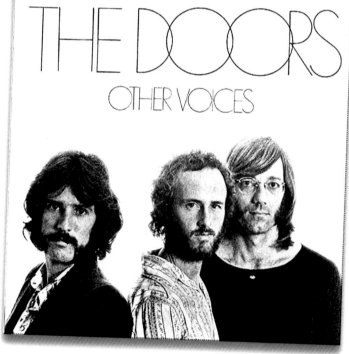

Right: *Other Voices*. Without Jim, it would have made sense to change the focus of things and head in a more progressive direction. 'Ships with Sails' would have been a good start. (*Rhino*)

Right: *Full Circle.* It has some real highlights and at least one stellar track that finally delivers on the jazz influence often claimed by various members of the band. (*Rhino*)

AN AMERICAN PRAYER

JIM MORRISON

MUSIC BY

THE DOORS

Left: *An American Prayer.* The remaining Doors saw it as a way to honour Jim's intention to be a poet. (*Elektra*)

Left: *Live At the Matrix 1967.* I love this album because it's The Doors when they were still a Hollywood garage band. (*Rhino*)

Right: *Live In Philadelphia 1970.* The sound quality is okay, and as this is in the same week as the Detroit show, the blues mood is here too.

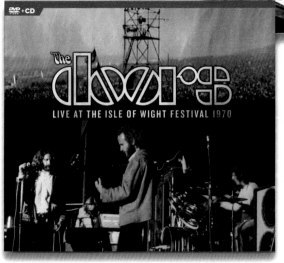

Left: *Live At The Isle Of Wight Festival 1970.* Ray Manzarek felt that Jim was in a sombre state, almost as though he was deliberately shutting down everything except his voice. (*Eagle Rock*)

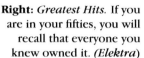

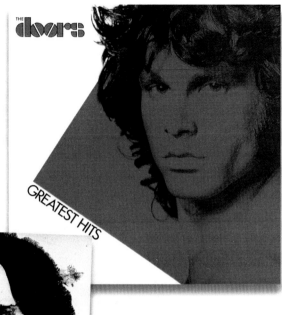

Right: *Greatest Hits.* If you are in your fifties, you will recall that everyone you knew owned it. *(Elektra)*

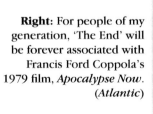

Left: *Weird Scenes Inside the Gold Mine.* It's a mix of singles, B-sides and 'deep cuts' that live up to the name and creepy album art. *(Rhino)*

Right: For people of my generation, 'The End' will be forever associated with Francis Ford Coppola's 1979 film, *Apocalypse Now.* *(Atlantic)*

Left: 'There can't be any large-scale revolution until there's a personal revolution, on an individual level.' Jim Morrison, in an interview in 1970. (*Tony Thompson*)

Below: 'No eternal reward will forgive us now for wasting the dawn.' Jim Morrison.

Morrison Hotel (1970)

Recorded: November 1969 – January 1970 at Elektra Sound West
Released: February 1970
Label: Elektra
Producer: Paul Rothchild
Engineer: Bruce Botnick
Additional Musicians: Ray Neapolitan (bass), Lonnie Brooks (bass), John Sebastian (harmonica)
Running Time: 37:47
Highest Chart Position: US: 4 UK: 12

David Fricke calls *Morrison Hotel* 'one of rock's great resurrection records, a striking fight for life by a band under attack.' It's hard to recapture just how out of favour The Doors were in 1969. They were no longer regarded as an innovative force in music. The small coterie of 'serious' rock critics of the time had, for the most part, hated *The Soft Parade*. In 1968, Jim Morrison had become a pinup and a regular in Tiger Beat magazine, but in the following year, his teeny-bopper audience had lost interest in him, particularly in the wake of the Miami incident. The counterculture didn't regard dropping one's trousers on stage as a particularly revolutionary act. They were now, as the saying went in the late '60s, 'nowhere, man'. When asked about the underground's dismissal of The Doors in an interview conducted just as they were starting this album, Jim said that they 'were the band people loved to hate'. He observed that they were 'universally despised' but that he 'relished' the situation. However, when he was asked if it bothered him, he said, 'Yeah, it does.' He then makes an interesting comparison with a novelist who has a critically acclaimed first book and then gets pummelled on his second. Jim's theory was that if they hung around a bit, people would come back to them. He was right!

Jim was facing serious jail time for indecent exposure and the band was having trouble finding concert dates. Promoters were understandably nervous about The Doors. Miami was only one of several concerts where things had got seriously out of hand on that tour.

By late 1969, it was not looking good for the band. If they had broken up then, no one would have been surprised or even cared much. A year, as I have noted before, was a long time in the late sixties. Popular culture was moving very fast. Woodstock had taken place in August, not long after the Manson murders, the moon landing, and the first email. One of the shows The Doors had played that year was the Toronto Rock and Roll Revival festival, where John Lennon had turned up and played a solo set with the hastily assembled Plastic Ono Band. While The Doors were recording *Morrison Hotel*, The Rolling Stones, in a generous decision to 'give back', held a free concert at the Altamont Speedway outside of San Francisco. It didn't go well.

F. Scott Fitzgerald famously observed, in the notes for his unfinished novel, *The Last Tycoon*, that 'there are no second acts in American life'. There are, of course, but they are very difficult to pull off. The Doors did it pretty convincingly with their final two studio records with Jim Morrison. They were never again as big as they were in 1967, but with *Morrison Hotel,* they revived the band and were once again taken seriously. If they had broken up in 1969 and not made *Morrison Hotel* and *L.A. Woman*, rock and roll would be poorer for it.

By the time the band decided to record again, the direction they had taken with *The Soft Parade* had been abandoned. Jac Holzman, the owner of Elektra, thought *Morrison Hotel* represented a move 'back to the roots' for The Doors. Too often, critics writing about this band ignore the fact that they were part of the music industry in America in the late 1960s and subject to the same influences and new directions as other acts. In 1968, The Band's *Music From Big Pink* had shaken the rock establishment to the core. Everything about that album appealed to the top echelon of musicians of the day. Bands got it together in the country and traded in their paisleys for plaid. Traffic, Fairport Convention, Eric Clapton, George Harrison, and many others were converted to an earthier sense of themselves as musicians. The Band's effect on rock and roll in the late sixties can't be overstated, and The Doors were not immune. Consciously or unconsciously, The Doors made a record in *Morrison Hotel* that reflected the same desire to strip back their sound to something essential.

That said, they did not do what might have been obvious – a more acoustic-oriented record with hints of country and early blues along the lines of *Beggars Banquet*. The other musical direction caught on this record is the one represented by bands like Canned Heat, Ten Years After, Led Zeppelin, and Johnny Winter. Blues rock was giving way to hard rock and there are hints of this on *Morrison Hotel*.

The album is divided up into two sides, 'Hard Rock Café' and 'Morrison Hotel'. These were both actual establishments in Los Angeles. Hard Rock Café was the sort of crummy Bukowski bar favoured by Jim, and Morrison Hotel offered low-end accommodation to the denizens of LA's skid row. The Hard Rock chain got its name from this album incidentally, not the other way around. Legendary rock photographer Henry Diltz did the cover shoot at Morrison Hotel very quickly after the day guy at the desk refused to allow the band to set up for a photoshoot. The Doors were looking for something akin to Diltz's cover of CSN's first album. It's never commented on, but I think there was something defiant about the band, including the name Morrison in the title of the record. A hundred other bands might have shied away from reminding everyone of the lead singer, who was up on indecent exposure charges, but The Doors put Jim front and centre.

Ray Manzarek says that Jim was relaxed and happy during the making of this record. Miami was not discussed, and Jim remained relatively sober throughout. It was made quickly and for a fraction of the cost of *The Soft*

Parade. Again, they had some trouble cobbling together material, but the result remains both compelling and mysterious in the best possible sense.

Side One
'Roadhouse Blues' (Morrison, The Doors)

If The Doors wanted to announce their intentions for this album, they chose the right song to get things rolling. 'Roadhouse Blues' remains one of the most exhilarating blues-based rock and roll songs. It has been covered by numerous anonymous bar bands playing in the sort of venue that the song honours. The 50th-anniversary edition of this album contains several takes, including the first where Jim explains the song:

> Gentlemens, gentlemens! Now the subject of this song is something all of you have seen one time or another. It's an old roadhouse, and we're down in the south or the Midwest, or maybe on the way to Bakersfield and we're driving in a 57 Chevy to an old roadhouse, you dig it? You know? It's about 1:30 and we're not driving too fast, but we're not driving too slow either. There's a sixpack of beer in the car and a few joints and we're listening to the radio, just driving to the old roadhouse, through nature.

The detail of the 57 Chevy is interesting. This car had already become iconic and identified with the nostalgia for the period which had already begun by 1969, and can be spotted in Sha Na Na's performance at Woodstock and in CCR's rockabilly classicism.

Early versions of the song were recorded with Ray singing on *The Soft Parade* sessions and there is a clip, with some very foggy footage, of the band playing it at the Seattle Pop Festival in July of 1969, more or less in the manner in which it would be recorded. It's an obvious live song and there are plenty of versions to hear. It was the opening song of the last show with Morrison in New Orleans.

This is speculative, but there is some idea that the roadhouse that Jim had in mind was more specific than his monologue might suggest. It is commonly thought that the Topanga Corral in Topanga Canyon was the subject of the song. The road up to it, Topanga Canyon Boulevard, snakes through the hills, so Jim's safe driving instructions (eyes on the road, hand upon the wheel) make sense. There is some idea that there were bungalows for rent out back. Some accounts even suggest that Jim owned a bungalow in the area. The Topanga Corral was a live venue that Linda Ronstadt, among others, played at early in their careers. It burned down in the early '70s.

There are numerous takes of 'Roadhouse Blues' to listen to, but the one that made it onto the album features two 'heavy' friends in Lonnie Mack and John Sebastian. Lonnie Mack had recorded a fiery RnB album in the early '60s called *The Wham Of That Memphis Man* that disappeared, like so much other great music, under the wave of the British invasion. By 1969, he was signed to Elektra and somehow ended up playing bass on this song in the absence of Ray

Neapolitan. Mack wasn't a bass player but was a superb guitar player and all-around musician, so he was more than up to the job. Some accounts suggest that Mack was admired by The Doors and that his presence took the session up a notch.

John Sebastian was the lead singer of the Lovin Spoonful, another band dogged in some ways by pop success. They were mishandled by their record company but produced a series of timeless singles. Sebastian's memorably stoned appearance in the *Woodstock* film would help to restore his credibility, but in late 1969 he was still under a cloud of a complicated story that linked him to the Spoonful's lead guitarist Zal Yanovsky's drug bust, where he supposedly gave up their dealer. On the song, he was credited as G. Puglese. Some accounts say that he did not want to be associated with The Doors after Miami, but this seems unlikely. He was signed to Kama Sutra as part of the Lovin Spoonful and Reprise as a solo artist. It seems more likely that it was just too much of a hassle for a few honks on the harp, as spectacular as they are. His father, John Sebastian Sr., is probably the most notable classical harmonica player in history, so junior was a good choice here. Jim, it has to be said, was a terrible harmonica player. Even if he did have the right key harp on hand, he seemed to have no idea what to do with it.

The Doors are on fire here, particularly Robby, whose guitar solo is astonishing. Ray's roadhouse piano creates exactly the right atmosphere, and Densmore plays it like it is Saturday night and the dancers need to hear that beat. Jim's blues voice is on full show here, picking up speed like a steam train. Lester Bangs, who didn't like the album but loved this song, said, in a review at the time, that it was 'one of the most convincing raunchy vocals Jim Morrison has ever recorded'.

It is a powerhouse of a song that has been covered by everyone from Status Quo to the neighbour whose band sometimes disturbs your quiet Saturday afternoon. It is the best sort of ragged blues rock song, but it is not altogether joyful. The final line strikes an uneasy and perhaps prophetic note: 'The future's uncertain and the end is always near.'

'Waiting For The Sun' (Morrison)

Clearly, this belongs on a different album, namely their third one, *Waiting For The Sun*. It was recorded then and is a better song than a handful of those that appeared on that record. The band wasn't happy with it, so they left it off the album while retaining the name. Yeah, I don't understand that either. It seems obvious that this comes from an earlier period. Everything from Jim's vocals to Robby's guitar style to the general sound mark it out as such. That said, it contributes to the somewhat eclectic nature of this album and provides a necessary breather between 'Roadhouse Blues' and 'You Make Me Real'. The lyrics are vaguely lysergic and hearken back to Jim's Venice days on the beach. There is seasonal imagery and the memorable line, 'This is the strangest life I've ever known.'

'You Make Me Real' (Morrison)

The Doors were in 'Get Back' mode here. This high-octane workout was part of their set at London Fog in 1966. The version on *Morrison Hotel* is not a radical departure from that version. David Fricke calls it 'garage blues napalm'. It's the sort of ragged frat rock thing that Rick & The Ravens specialised in, and the type of 'keep 'em dancing' rock and roll song that people like Billy Lee Riley cranked out at the Whisky before Love and The Doors turned up. The lyrics are fairly standard sexual attraction stuff with a few Morrison gems like, 'So let me slide in your tender sunken sea' scattered throughout.

It's not one of their great songs, which makes one wonder why anyone thought, on an album featuring so many great tracks, that it should be the only single from the album. 'Roadhouse Blues' was on the flipside in what must be one of the greatest lopsided A-side / B-side stories in rock and roll history. Not surprisingly, it drifted around the lower end of the *Billboard* Top 100 for a while, before peaking at number 50. Listen to this whole album and consider what songs you would release as singles. Would this make the cut?

'Peace Frog' (Morrison, Kreiger)

The slightly absurd title aside, it is one of The Doors' greatest moments. The mystifying decision not to release it as a single did not stop radio hosts from playing it, usually letting it drift into the mellower 'Blue Sunday', which follows it on the LP. It did not appear on *13*, the original greatest hits album that was released before *L.A. Woman* but was on *Weird Scenes Inside The Goldmine*, which appeared in 1972. It was decades before it turned up on another 'greatest hits' package. It remains a great favourite of Doors fans and, intriguingly, a song often admired by those who are otherwise immune to this band's charms.

With all due respect to Robby's songwriting which, of course, secured the band's status as a top act in the late '60s, and probably for a long time to come, it seems to me that their finest moments were more collaborative. The band would develop one of their irresistible grooves and Jim would get out his notebooks. This is essentially the story of 'Peace Frog'. As Robby has mentioned in interviews, the song was in place and Jim supplied lyrics in the studio. An instrumental version can be heard on various live recordings from 1969.

Robby begins with a slightly wah wah'd vamp on a G5 chord and is joined in succession by John Densmore and Ray Neapolitan on funky bass. Neapolitan, who plays bass on all but two tracks on this album, had played with the Don Ellis Orchestra and would go on to play with John Lennon, Leonard Cohen, Dion, Joe Cocker, and many others. Later in 1970, he played bass on John Sebastian's first solo album. I wonder if they discussed *Morrison Hotel*!

Jim's lyrics were drawn from a poem he had written called 'Abortion Stories'. The song, with its repeated images of blood, is political, social, and possibly personal. There is 'Blood in the street / The town of Chicago', a reference to the riots at the Democratic Convention in that city in the summer of 1968, and 'Blood in the streets / In the town of New Haven', where Jim had his own showdown with the man in the same year. Jim's sense of revolution was closer to the Beat philosophy of freedom than any strict political agenda. His witty contention that The Doors were 'erotic politicians' speaks to a much broader idea of change. Morrison's vision in this song takes in the political but also touches on the character of a woman who 'drove away / Sunlight in her hair' and the blood that, 'stains the roofs / And the palm trees of Venice'. There is a reference to a 'terrible summer', and 'Fantastic LA'. Assuming that some of this was drawn from material written during Jim's magic summer of 1965, this might be a reference to the Watts riots of that same summer. It's not hard to imagine Jim on the roof watching the red glow of burning buildings to the southeast and conjuring images of blood.

Then there is the brief interlude where Jim interjects with a fragment from a strange childhood memory. When Jim was nearly four, in 1947, his family was driving through the desert in New Mexico and came across a car accident involving a group of Native Americans. The young Jim was, not surprisingly, was upset by the sight. As a young man, he told the story regularly with the implication that somehow he had absorbed the soul of one of the victims.

> Indians scattered on dawn's highway bleeding
> Ghosts crowd the young child's fragile eggshell mind

This sequence will appear again in 'Ghost Song' on *American Prayer,* but it's an intriguing interlude here. Jim had a vague fascination with Native Americans, and there is perhaps something logical about this reference to the original inhabitants of America in a song about the nation's inherent violence.

It should also be noted that Robby's guitar solo is brilliant. I sense that there was a shift in his playing at some point during 1969 – perhaps he just had more time to practice after all of their gigs were cancelled – and he is playing lead much more confidently from this period. This is just one of the incendiary solos on this record.

'Blue Sunday' (Morrison)

If you first heard this song on *Weird Scenes Inside The Goldmine*, you would have assumed that it was the second part of 'Peace Frog'. Indeed, on the sleeve of that collection, they are listed as 'Peace Frog/Blue Sunday'. They seem to have always been a pair. The 'Peace Frog' instrumental on the *Live At The Aquarius Theatre* recordings, and others, leads into 'Blue Sunday'. Yet, they are different songs, and it is worth considering this one on its own merits.

John Densmore says, rather wittily, in his memoir, that 'Blue Sunday' is 'Frank Sinatra meets Carlos Castenada'. It's a pretty apt description. Jim certainly croons the hell out of this song, but it has a slightly mystical feel which is mainly attributable to Robby's guitar work. He dabbles in one of his flamenco scales and ensures that the Castenada aspect is never overwhelmed by Ol' Blue Eyes.

It's a love song and most people think that Pamela Courson was the subject.

'Ship Of Fools' (Morrison, Kreiger)

There are a lot of ships and a lot of fools. It would be easier to list the bands that haven't recorded a song called 'Ship Of Fools', but the list of those who have, includes The Grateful Dead, Bob Seger, World Party and Erasure. The Doors may have been the first, however. The phrase is drawn from Plato and is the title of a famous painting by Hieronymus Bosch. It is likely, however, that Jim was inspired by the title of a 1965 film starring the rather unlikely combination of Lee Marvin and Vivien Leigh. It was based on a bestselling 1962 novel about a sea voyage by Katherine Anne Porter. The story is an elaborate metaphor for the rise of fascism. Morrison may or may not have seen the film or read the book. The phrase itself is rich with possibilities and his take is a compelling one.

There are a couple of songs in The Doors catalogue where Morrison touches on what was then known as ecology and the real possibility that the Earth was in danger. Rachel Carson's landmark study, *Silent Spring*, had appeared earlier in the decade and, not long before *Morrison Hotel* was recorded, a benefit concert for the newly founded Greenpeace occurred in Vancouver. To what extent Jim was aware of the budding environmental movement isn't clear, but in several instances in his songwriting, there are references to this topic.

The other factor that informs this song is the new consciousness of the planet, seen from outer space, and the moon landing in the summer of 1969. Actual space travel had a profound effect on songwriters and there are many references to space in the popular music of this period.

'Ship Of Fools' opens with a riff reminiscent of Ray Charles' 'What I Say'. There is some interesting, almost Prog-like interplay between Ray, Ray Neapolitan and Robby throughout the song.

This is yet another song about ships from the admiral's son, but who is Captain Goodtrips? His father? Jerry Garcia? Neil Armstrong? A West Hollywood dealer?

Side Two

'Land Ho!' (Morrison, Kreiger)

And we're back at sea! Lyrically, this is an unusual song for Jim, a sort of sea shanty in ballad metre with rhyming couplets here and there. It is not a well-known track and it is rarely referred to by the band's various biographers. I wonder if it comes from an early poem of Jim's, inspired by his father's stories. A psychologist would have a field day with the numerous mentions of the sea and sailing in Jim's writing.

The opening is a classic pre-war blues riff. John Densmore does mention in his memoir that he played a 'skiffle' beat on this one. Robby is in fine form here, as is Ray Manzarek. The best part is the stop towards the middle of the song, where Jim hollers 'Land Ho!' Robby's guitar solo at the end is a highlight and further evidence of his growing confidence as a lead player.

'The Spy' (Morrison)

'The Spy' is built on a slightly creepy blues riff from Robby. It's not miles away from something like Howlin' Wolf's 'Smokestack Lightning' in tempo. Ray's honky-tonk piano fills some of the space wonderfully as Jim croons ominously about knowing 'your deepest, secret fear'. Towards the end of the song, he hits some of the lowest notes of his career, sounding more like Fred Neil than Sinatra.

Like 'Ship Of Fools', the title came from a novel. This time, the author was the French writer Anaïs Nin, someone Jim probably had read and was certainly familiar with as one of the great bohemian figures of the 20th century. She is somewhat forgotten today but was once a celebrated author and essayist. Her frank interrogations of sexuality and freedom would have appealed to Jim. The song has nothing to do with the novel beyond sharing a title, but it is an interesting connection. Anaïs Nin was a friend and lover of Henry Miller, one of the many American writers in whose footsteps Jim made his way to Paris in 1971.

The blues riff would have made 'The Spy' a strong live song, but it was only played a handful of times in 1970. The Long Beach version, which can be heard online, is pretty faithful to the recorded track, but a couple of months later in Boston, it's starting to swing a bit at a slightly faster tempo. At that show, Morrison adds a spoken word coda where he accuses the subject of infidelity and says that he 'knows you've been BAD.'

'Queen of the Highway' (Morrison, Kreiger)

This is a wonderful track that is arguably another 'deep cut' from *Morrison Hotel*. It's a classic Morrison road trip story and a vision of an American hippie couple in Eden. John Densmore was disappointed by the band's performance. He said that he thought, in this instance, they had let Jim down. I think it's one of the stronger tracks on the record. Ray is in great form on electric piano, and Ray Neapolitan's solid bass work holds things together nicely. It's hard to understand what Densmore regrets here, but as it was never done live, it seems that no one was entirely happy with the version on the album.

Possibly, they felt that despite many attempts, they couldn't get it right. The rock critic Greil Marcus says it sounds like a group of musicians that 'don't trust themselves'. Marcus, in his book on the band, *The Doors: A Lifetime Of Listening In Five Mean Years* (2011), devotes an entire chapter to an outtake, presumably the 'jazz' version which appears on *The Doors: Box Set*. He says that this is a glimpse of The Doors in a mode that he likens to Geoff Dyer's vision of Chet Baker in *But Beautiful*, his collection of fictional portraits of jazz greats. They are in the 'cool' zone, playing without all of the weight of stardom and image'. Dyer says that Baker played as though he was waving goodbye to each note. Marcus suggests that The Doors, particularly Manzarek, are doing that here.

In his memoir, Manzarek seems to be remembering this version rather than the one on the album. He writes: 'Imagine yourself at a smoky jazz joint in the village circa 1962 with Jim as a world-weary existential balladeer singing a tale of love.'

'Indian Summer' (Morrison, Kreiger)

In 1987, this song was covered by Hope Sandoval and David Roback in their pre-Mazzy Star band, Opal. The band, presumably named for the Syd Barrett album, sound like they are channelling the Velvet Underground, and yet what they capture is the haunting quality of The Doors' original, an understated gem of a song. The lyrics sound unfinished, but there is something mesmerising about them as they are repeated.

> I love you, the best
> Better than all the rest
> That I meet in the summer
> Indian summer

This recording by The Doors is a very early one, their first as a four-piece according to John Densmore. There was a version recorded the same day as 'Moonlight Drive' in August 1966, and another recorded in September. It's not clear which one appears on *Morrison Hotel*. Since at least *Waiting For The Sun*, the band seemed to have had trouble finding new material, but this is an interesting choice. Sonically, it is very different to the songs recorded in late '69 and early 1970, but it works well on the album as a mysterious detour back to an earlier period before 'Maggie McGill', another blues rock example of the new direction.

'Maggie M'Gill' (Morrison, The Doors)

Possibly to signal their new direction, The Doors abandoned the practice of finishing their albums with a big concept song and instead closed with this rough-hewn, medium-tempo blues shouter.

Robby straps on the slide here for decorative bits and a great solo over the main riff. Lonnie Mack provides some further stunning bass work over Densmore's ever solid timekeeping. It's a cool tune and one that was a frequent addition to their remaining live shows, including the final one with Jim in New Orleans.

The lyrics sound as though they might have been improvised originally. It starts as the story of the titular character becoming a prostitute in an Old West scenario. There is a rather interesting couplet:

> Illegitimate son of a rock n' roll star
> Mom met dad in the back of a rock n' roll car, yeah

And the final:

> Well, I'm an old bluesman and I think that you understand
> I've been singing the blues ever since the world began

Jim delivers it all powerfully and convincingly. It's not a particularly profound song, except that Maggie M'Gill heads to a place called 'Tangie Town'. There is no such town, and a 'tangie' is a figure out of Scottish folklore. It is not clear if he meant to give the song a slightly mythical bent, but it is an intriguing possibility. The tangie is a sea horse which might be a link to 'Horse Latitudes' and the watery corner of Jim's imagination. It might also be something else entirely! In any case, 'Maggie M'Gill' reaffirms the shift back to blues for The Doors, something that they will explore further on their final studio album with Jim, *LA Woman*.

Related Songs
'I Will Never Be Untrue' (Morrison)
This Jimmy Reed style slow blues doesn't seem to have gone much further than a take or two, but it is worth hearing, as it is another indication that they were revisiting classic blues on this album. It is done as an appealing eight bar-style blues and one can't help wishing that they had finished it. It appears on concert recordings from the period.

'Rock Me Baby' (Waters)
This blues standard was part of their set at London Fog and appears on the 2016 release of those early live recordings. It is a song they returned to regularly over the years on stage and they seem to have considered it for both this album and the one that follows.

'Money (That's What I Want)' (Bradford, Gordy)
This is indeed the early Motown hit for Barrett Strong written by Berry Gordy himself. It was covered by everyone in the sixties but most notably by The Beatles. However, the inspiration here might be John Lee Hooker's stunning version from his wonderful 1966 album, *It Serves You Right To Suffer*, a record of dark blues that one can easily imagine appealing to The Doors. It doesn't seem to have ever been a serious consideration for inclusion on this album, but it might point ahead to the Hooker cover on *L.A. Woman*.

Absolutely Live (1970)

Recorded: Various concerts 1969-1970
Released: July 1970
Label: Elektra
Producer: Paul Rothchild
Engineer: Bruce Botnick
Running Time: 72:02
Highest Chart Position: US: 8, UK: 69

In 1970, the live rock and roll album was still a relatively recent phenomenon. However, there was no shortage of them, and around the time that *Absolutely Live* was released, the soon to be common practice of using them to fill in gaps between studio albums and as a means of fulfilling contractual obligations was already in play. Paul Rothchild admitted as much in a later interview, where he suggested that they only released this one because it had been six months since *Morrison Hotel* and that some new product was required to maintain interest in the band.

A Doors concert album was a great idea. The band's reputation as a live act was considerable and controversial. Miami was a personal disaster for Jim and a devastating blow to the band, but there is, as they say, no such thing as bad publicity. It's worth remembering that rock and roll as theatre was something that very few bands engaged in at that point. The Grateful Dead and other San Francisco acts had experimented with extended jams and free form improvisation, but mainly on their instruments. Jim was taking rock and roll in a direction suggested by the Beat poets a decade earlier. Concerts were not, for Jim, simply a place to promote the latest Doors single or provide some entertainment. A Doors show was a spectacle, a mass meeting, and a gathering of the tribes. Jim said once that he was 'exploring the bounds of reality'. In their shows, he was exploring the bounds of the rock and roll live event, and he certainly pushed those boundaries. This might be the real legacy of The Doors.

That doesn't mean, unfortunately, that this is a great record. But then, live albums are rarely great. As a sub-genre, they are a hit and miss affair. It's easy to think of the exceptions, the truly brilliant live albums, but for every *Get Yer Ya's Out!* there are ten *Love You Lives*. *Absolutely Live* is well worth owning and has some stellar moments, but like so many live records, it is a bit disappointing.

It is also not a true document of a Doors show in any sense. In the last few years, Rhino Records has released many complete live shows by The Doors, including some very early concerts and the various '69/'70 shows from which the material on *Absolutely Live* was drawn. Many of these are outstanding and give a much clearer picture of the band on stage. However, *Absolutely Live* was the only official Doors live release until the appearance of *Alive She Cried* in 1983 and the only one released in Jim Morrison's lifetime. Thus, despite being

supplanted by more representative material, it remains an important part of
The Doors' story.

Jim Morrison did not like the cover of the original LP. He had gone to great
pains to change his image and here he was, clean-shaven, leather panted, and
slim on the front of their new album. Six months later, Elektra did the same
thing on *13*, a greatest hits collection.

The reviews were lukewarm. *Rolling Stone*, generally not well disposed
towards the band in the '60s, ran a review by Gloria Vanjuk that poured
scorn on the album while admitting that it had a few good moments. 'The
Celebration Of The Lizard', appearing in full for the first time here, was
'rancid', and 'Universal Mind' was 'mediocre'. She was not impressed with
Jim's improvised raps, labelling them 'juvenile' and 'drunken'. There's no
question that the album is flawed, but it is nowhere as bad as Vanjuk suggests.
Another example, perhaps, of Jim's sense that they had somehow become 'the
band you love to hate'. Subsequent reviews have been better. Robert Christgau,
not a great fan of the band, noted correctly that it is well recorded. Recording
The Doors in the barns they played on that tour would have presented a real
challenge. Listen to Cream's live tracks on *Goodbye Cream* for evidence of just
how hard it was in those days to capture a band's sound in a large venue.

Side One
'Who Do You Love?' (McDaniels)
The album begins with the house announcer trying to get everyone back
to their seats. He's using his Chip Monck at Woodstock voice. 'Everything's
beautiful, man, just sit down!'

'Who Do You Love?' is a warhorse of a song that has been recorded by
hundreds, if not thousands, of acts. The original version was released by its
author, Bo Diddley, in 1956 on Chess Records' subsidiary, Checker. Ronnie
Hawkins recorded it in 1963. His version is notable for the young Robbie
Robertson's killer guitar solo, which he recreated when The Band performed it
with the rockabilly singer at their final show, known as *The Last Waltz*, in 1976.

The Doors' version does not follow any particular arrangement. It's likely
that it was a song that went back to Rick & The Ravens and was never far
from their live sets. Quicksilver Messenger Service, a band The Doors shared
bills with, performed and recorded a well-known version. The Blues Project
featured it on their *Live At The Café A Go Go* album. Robby seems to have been
a fan of guitarist Danny Kalb, so he would have known this version.

It works well as the first song on the record. John Densmore sounds the
tribal drums before Ray Manzarek comes in with a bass line and Robby Kreiger
breaks out the slide. If you are familiar with the record, you might be surprised
that it was actually deep into the set of their first show at the Felt Forum in
New York in January 1970, from which this recording was drawn. They'd just
finished 'Five To One' and were about to launch into 'Little Red Rooster'!

At the risk of sounding like the *Rolling Stone* reviewer, Jim sounds a bit less than committed here. The band is on fire, but Jim comes up a bit short. He sounds uncharacteristically tired. It's only at the end of the song that he brings out his blues belter voice. There are plenty of live versions of 'Who Do You Love?' by The Doors that you can listen to for comparison's sake. He inhabits the story a bit more on the *Live At The Matrix* version from 1967.

It's a creepy song involving reptiles, so a good fit for The Doors all around.

'Alabama Song (Whiskey Bar)'
A surprisingly faithful version of an early album track from the same New York show as 'Who Do You Love?', this is a welcome, if brief, interlude between two blues covers. Jim loses his way right at the end but is in good voice.

'Back Door Man'
Another track from their first album, 'Back Door Man' doesn't break any new ground but still sounds pretty good. This recording is from the second New York show and features a blistering guitar solo from Robby. Again, Jim sounds a little bored.

'Love Hides' (Morrison)
This sounds like an improv over the end of 'Back Door Man', and it is, except that this version is drawn from the Philadelphia show on the tour. It's essentially a list of places where love hides, but Jim delivers it all with flair. It's more of a fragment than a song, but it is worth hearing.

'Five To One'
Paul Rothchild returns seamlessly to the second New York show for a solid version of this live staple for the band. This is Jim's best performance thus far on the record, and Robby is stunning, as he is on most tracks here.

Side Two
'Build Me A Woman' (Morrison)
No need for Rothchild's edits here; this did indeed follow 'Five To One' at the second New York show. It's another twelve-bar blues workout with a series of fragmentary lyrics, none of which are particularly interesting unless you think 'I've got the poontang blues down to my cowboy shoes' is clever. Sometimes this is noted as a highlight of the record. Not for me.

'When The Music's Over'
The closer from their second album is given a big workout here later in the set of the second New York show. Considering how many times Jim had probably sung this one, he performs it with conviction and care. I suppose there is something poignant about the 'Before I go into the big sleep' section when one realises that this young man only had another 18 months or so on earth.

About halfway through the song, he shrieks 'shut up' and asks, 'now is that any way to behave at a rock and roll show?' He sounds like he is enjoying himself and, despite *Rolling Stone*'s review, sober and at ease. This prefaces a wonderfully trippy instrumental section where Ray steps out with Robby before Jim comes back and says, rather wittily, 'Well, that's New York for you, the only people who rush the stage are guys.' A highlight of the album for sure.

Side Three
'Close To You' (Dixon)
'Ahh, ladies and gentlemen, I don't know if you realise it, but tonight you are in for a special treat.' The crowd cheers and Jim says, 'no, not that, you only get THAT treat on full moons', before making a specific reference to Miami with 'the last time it happened, grown men cried and policemen handed in their badges'. The treat, it turns out, is a lead vocal from Ray on blues standard, 'Close To You'. By this stage, Ray had become quite adept at imitating Jim so that he could finish the shows when his lead singer was absent, drunk, in jail, or all three. You can hear elements of his take on Jim's blues voice here. Jim chimes in on the chorus.

'Universal Mind' (Morrison, Kreiger)
'Universal Mind' is the only fully formed new song on this album. It's a great tune and one wonders why it only appears here. The lyrics are witty, and Jim delivers them with great warmth. 'Then you came along with a suitcase and a song.' If this is indeed a newer set of lyrics from Morrison, he seems to have drifted into a franker style. The wider philosophical ideas remain – the universal mind, but 'I was turning keys, I was setting people free' almost sounds like Leonard Cohen. By 1970, when *Absolutely Live* was released, the singer-songwriter phenomenon was well underway. There is, I believe, in this song a hint of Jim Morrison as a notional solo act in the early '70s. Alas, we'll never know, but this remains a highlight of this album and their career in general. The recording comes from a Hollywood show at the Aquarius Theatre in July 1969, around the time that *The Soft Parade* album was released.

'Petition the Lord with Prayer/Dead Cats/Break On Through 2' (Morrison, The Doors)
The crowd in New York roars when Jim begins his 'Petition The Lord With Prayer' sermon. Paul Rothchild then takes us to Detroit, where Jim riffs on dead cats in top hats to the tune of 'Break On Through' before launching into the actual song. It's not a particularly remarkable performance, but it is done as something of a duet with Ray and is filled with a garage punk urgency that would certainly have appealed in the city of the Stooges and the MC5. Robby stretches out with another top solo before Ray and Jim chomp through a final verse to finish side three.

Side Four
'The Celebration Of The Lizard'

Thrilling. I have covered this piece or series of pieces in the section on *Waiting For The Sun,* but any lingering doubt about this as one of Morrison's finest moments should be extinguished by this performance at the Aquarius Theatre in Hollywood in July 1969. Keeping in mind that this was only the fourth show they had played since Miami, Jim is in remarkable form on this recording. The band creates an elaborate soundscape for the various stories and Morrison doesn't miss a beat. Considering that 'The Celebration of the Lizard' was something they had recorded but not, for the most part, used on a previous album, they all sound committed to it. The original *Rolling Stone* review felt that this was something you would only listen to once. I couldn't disagree more. I've owned this album in one format or another for 40 years and have always regarded it as a centrepiece. Live albums are disappointing when they seem to feature little except for underplayed, overlong versions of the band's best songs. This is an example of what live albums do best. The decision to include this instead of, say, 'The End' was a masterstroke on Rothchild's part.

'Soul Kitchen'

The temptation to finish the album with 'Hello, I Love You' or one of their other chart hits must have been enormous. Instead, side four closes with another track from the 1969 Aquarius shows, a 'deep cut' from their first album, and one of their finest songs. The version here is a little slower, a little funkier. Ray sounds more like Booker T. Jones than Eric Burdon now on organ, and Robby has become a far more confident guitar player in the years since the release of the first album. It cooks along, doesn't outstay its welcome and is an appropriate closer to an album, which despite its flaws, remains a snapshot of the band in the process of reinventing itself for a new decade.

'L.A. Woman' (1971)

Recorded: December 70 – January 71 at The Doors Workshop, 8512 Santa Monica Blvd
Released: April 1971
Label: Elektra
Producers: Bruce Botnick and The Doors
Engineer: Bruce Bortnick
Additional musicians: Marc Benno (guitar), Jerry Scheff (bass guitar)
Running Time: 48:24
Highest Chart Position: US:9, UK: 28

Not many bands produce a final album that rivals the best of their early work. Especially not bands like The Doors. When they began recording it in late December 1970, Jim Morrison was facing a six-month prison sentence in Florida. His alcohol intake was astronomic, and he was becoming fonder and fonder of cocaine, according to some accounts. His health was poor, and, by his own admission, he no longer wrote, read, or did much of anything.

Only days before they went into the studio, they had played what would be the last Doors show with Jim Morrison at The Warehouse in New Orleans. The venue was already legendary, but Ray Manzarek found it sinister. 'A packed warehouse on the docks. Low, dark, and ancient. Slave vibes, juju vibes, Marie Laveau, and Dr John walking on gilded splinters.' It sounds like the perfect setting for a Doors show, but it was not a great night. Jim lost interest, or as Ray saw it, his spirit was 'streaming up from his stomach and out through his crown chakra. Out into that voodoo night'. There is a rough recording available of the show and it sounds chaotic. John Densmore was furious and vowed never to play on stage with Jim again. According to Manzarek, a decision was made when they returned to LA that The Doors would stop touring. An observer at the time might have concluded that The Doors had been on borrowed time for a while and that they were now effectively finished as a band.

Certainly, their producer, Paul Rothchild thought so. His departure, as recording for *L.A. Woman* began, was unexpected and dramatic. The story is that he listened to early versions of the songs, 'L.A. Woman' and 'Riders On The Storm'. He thought they were good but that the band was not in any shape to play them properly. After a week with the band in the studio, he decided that he'd had enough of The Doors generally, and Jim Morrison in particular. He declared that 'Love Her Madly' (some accounts say 'Riders On The Storm') sounded like 'cocktail music' and walked out. The story is, as they say, complicated. He had produced *Pearl* for Janis Joplin earlier in the year. He had formed an intense working relationship with her and found the experience enormously rewarding. But then Janis had died in October of 1971. This incident with The Doors seems to have taken place in November of that year. It's not hard to imagine that Rothchild was in no condition to produce anyone, least of all a band seemingly on its last legs. The Doors were upset but decided to press on with Bruce Botnick as their producer.

Ray Manzarek suggests that the decision to stop touring took some of the pressure off the band. Jim had been sentenced to six months for indecent exposure and related charges but had immediately appealed. No one had any idea what would happen next except that Jim was planning to go to Paris when they finished recording. He had been warned that he might have to surrender his passport at the next hearing. No one, including Jim, seemed to think that the band was breaking up, so this is not The Doors' *Abbey Road*, a farewell album. Indeed, The Doors minus Jim were back in the studio in the spring of 1971, rehearsing and creating tracks for the next album with their lead singer in mind.

Bruce Botnick's masterstroke was moving the sessions to The Doors Workshop, a space where the band rehearsed on Santa Monica Blvd. He brought over the very eight-track board they had used on *Strange Days* and created a vocal booth for Jim Morrison in the bathroom. Somehow, being out of the studio environment breathed life into both singer and band. According to Ray and John, the songs came together naturally and holistically. Jim drew on his famous notebooks, but there were new songs too. 'L'America' had been recorded earlier, as will be discussed, and some of these songs, like Texas Radio, had been played live for a while, but the bulk of this material was fresh.

Two musicians were added for the sessions. Jerry Scheff, who had played the distinctive bassline on The Association's 'Along Comes Mary' and was a member of Elvis Presley's band at the time, plays on almost every song here. Jim Morrison was reportedly enthusiastic at the idea of playing with a member of Elvis' band. Scheff would go on to play with many artists but is almost always noted for his work on *L.A. Woman*. The other musician was guitarist Marc Benno. This was the first time The Doors had used a second guitar player, and Benno was an interesting choice. He had played in the Asylum Choir with Leon Russell before starting a solo career in the same year he worked with The Doors. In 1972, he would release the magisterial *Ambush* album, one of the great records that not enough people have heard. He liked working with Jim and remembered him as a 'wild gorilla' in the studio, with a mic and a telephone book of lyrics.

The album was recorded in about nine days and done mainly live. John Densmore calls it a 'punk album' in his memoir. Jim Morrison saw it as a 'blues album'. The Doors' young manager Bill Siddons who was sitting upstairs in the office while it was being made, called it 'visceral' and 'close to the bone'. Ray Manzarek said that the album 'just fucking exploded in the studio'. Robby Kreiger's work on the record is outstanding and he too seems to have only good memories of the brief sessions.

It was well-received at the time. Robert Meltzer's 1971 review in *Rolling Stone* is somewhat sardonic in tone, but he declares it their best album. He feels that the band had never sounded so together. The Doors were, by the time it was released in April of 1971, already considered relics of another era. However, they were still a popular band with record buyers, and the album reached the top ten of *Billboard*'s album charts and 28 in the UK. Considering the riches of rock and roll in 1971 and the fact that there was no tour support, this was no small achievement. 'L.A. Woman's stature has grown over the years and it is now commonly considered a 'classic' album. Along with their first album, it featured on *Rolling Stone*'s 500 Greatest Albums list when it was originally compiled in 2003.

Side One
'The Changeling' (The Doors)
In the tradition of solid opening tracks, 'The Changeling' is a soul-influenced stomper and one of the band's great lesser-known tracks. It opens with a Junior Walker and the All-Stars style bass and drums combination before Ray joins in Booker T. mode. Then Robby appears playing a Jimmy Nolen style guitar riff. If 'Roadhouse Blues' evokes the Chicago blues of the 1950s, 'The Changeling' is a celebration of 1960s rhythm and blues. Jim Morrison samples Aretha Franklin's 1967 smash hit 'Chain Of Fools', swapping her 'chain chain chain' for 'change change change'.

The lyrics came out of an old notebook, but it is hard not to hear a line like 'but I've never been so broke that I couldn't leave town' and not think about his imminent departure. There is no suggestion that he knew he only had limited time left to live, but there are a lot of goodbyes on the album. He left in March of 1971 while the album was being mixed.

The title was inspired by a student film by one of his classmates at UCLA. In some European traditions, the 'changeling' was a human child that had been replaced by a fairy child. The myth probably grew from children born with physical or neurological differences, but it is an enduring story in many countries. Jim is using it ironically here in a song that repeats the word 'change', but it was probably a story that appealed to him.

This is one of a handful of the songs on this album that was played live. A rough recording of the first of two shows in Dallas, their third last with Jim, features a more or less complete version of the song.

'Love Her Madly' (The Doors)
In the '80s/'90s Canadian television comedy show *Kids In The Hall*, there is a skit set in a record store where a customer shows some interest in The Doors and is lectured by the fanatical shop clerk about what it is to be a Doors fan. When the customer says that he likes 'Love Her Madly', the clerk says, 'If you're a Doors fan, you don't like that song.' Certainly, Paul Rothchild didn't like it. In an interview ten years after the album was released, he said: 'That's exactly the song I was talking about that I said sounded like cocktail music. THAT'S the song that drove me out of the studio. That it sold a million copies means nothing to me. It's still bad music'.

So what's wrong with Love Her Madly? Nothing that I can hear, but it is indeed the most pop thing they had recorded since *The Soft Parade's* 'Touch Me'. It was another Robby Kreiger composition and another hit record. It came very close to being another top ten hit for them in the US and is on all of the various greatest hits collections. The lyrics are, as someone said at the time, another of Robby's 'isn't my girlfriend crazy?' songs. It's not particularly profound, but the idea of the singer loving her even 'when she's walking out the door' is clever and memorable. Robby, interviewed years later in a guitar magazine, said that he wrote it on a Gibson 335 12 string one night after his partner Lynn had stormed out, slamming the door so hard that the house shook.

One thing it doesn't sound like is 'cocktail music'. Jerry Scheff's bass work is stunning and should be heard properly with good headphones. The whole band sounds great here, really, and it's a good argument against the idea that they were finished. Jim's voice had perhaps lost some of its youthful power, but it had become more weathered and world-weary. As always, his timing is impeccable, and he tells the story with great conviction.

This is another original from *L.A. Woman* that the band tried out at the early show of their penultimate concert date with Jim in Dallas in December of 1970. It's well worth hearing because the song sounds far more blues-oriented here. Without Scheff's bass work in the live setting, it sounds far more like The Doors as they were circa 1970. If this was more or less what they played for Paul Rothchild, it's a little hard to understand why he threw up his hands and walked out. Once again, it doesn't seem to have had much to do with the music.

'Been Down So Long' (The Doors)

During the recording of *L.A. Woman*, Jim declared that one particular day in the studio would be 'blues day' whereupon they would record blues songs. This one, which had been in their live set sporadically throughout the year, is perhaps the strongest of the material. Again, Jerry Scheff's bass work is a key element. He and John Densmore provided a rock-solid rhythm section for Robby, Jim, and what sounds like a second guitarist, Marc Benno. Robby's distinctive slide work is on show here and Jim is in great voice. As the song develops, the intensity of his delivery seems to grow so that by the end, he is hollering. It's a thrilling performance.

On a live version from one of the April 1970 Boston shows, Ray is on guitar while Robby plays bass! Since Ray's keyboard work doesn't appear on the song, he may be on one of the several guitar tracks that can be heard on the recording.

The song shares its hook phrase with a 1966 novel by Richard Farina. While the song does not have anything else to do with the book, Farina may have been of interest to Jim Morrison. He was, in the early and mid-sixties, associated with Bob Dylan as the husband of Joan Baez's sister, Mimi. Richard and Mimi recorded a couple of albums together before his death in a motorcycle crash not long after his book was published. Richard, a close friend of the now reclusive novelist Thomas Pynchon, was essentially a literary figure who dabbled in music. Morrison may have taken some interest in his career as he contemplated his own desire to be taken seriously as a writer.

The phrase 'I've been down so long that it looks like up to me' is an old blues trope that appears in the Memphis musician Furry Lewis' 1928 recording 'I Will Turn Your Money Green'.

The other aspect of the song that is of interest is the 'warden, warden, warden' verse. Jim was still facing six months in a maximum-security prison, barring a successful appeal. The reference to jail may not have been accidental.

'Cars Hiss By My Window' (The Doors)

This is another recording from 'blues day', and though not one as enthralling as 'Been Down So Long', it remains a much loved 'deep cut' on this album. The lyrics are drawn from Jim's prolific summer of 1965. Ray says that Jim told him that it was about 'living in Venice Beach in a hot room with a hot girlfriend, with an open window, in a bad time'. Presumably, these are some of the same cars that appear in 'Soul Kitchen', 'crawling past stuffed with eyes'.

An early version of the song appears on an album released by Rhino called *Backstage And Dangerous: A Private Rehearsal,* a recording of a 1969 rehearsal at the Aquarius Theatre in between the two shows that they played there in that year. It begins with a line or two that will appear in 'The Changeling' before becoming this song. Robby plays Robert Johnson style blues guitar while John keeps time.

The recording that appears on the album seems a bit unfinished, with Jim providing a vocal imitation of a wah-wah guitar solo and something else that sounds like his rendering of a harmonica part. It's charming and helps to maintain the casual atmosphere of the album but does not, perhaps, reward repeated listens. That said, it seems to have been part of the song, as he does the same thing in an alternative version.

In the original *Rolling Stone* review, Robert Meltzer makes an intriguing comparison with another enigmatic Los Angeles artist of the time: 'Just check out 'Cars Hiss By My Window', compare it to the half-assed blues attempts of fellow Southern Californian Captain Beefheart and see who's got the greater vestige of potentially galling pretentiously indulgent self-esteem. (If you don't admit it's the noble Captain, then you can't have much of a sense of either humour or fair play.)' I'm not sure how one measures 'potentially galling pretentiously indulgent self-esteem', but it is a reminder that The Doors did not exist in a vacuum and that they were living and making music in the same universe, the same city even, as someone like Beefheart.

'L.A. Woman' (The Doors)

There is no doubt that the title track is one of the great songs by this band. Robby calls it the 'quintessential Doors song'. Ray Manzarek regularly noted it as his favourite track by the band in interviews over the years. It has remained a staple of FM rock radio for decades and is, along with 'Light My Fire', probably the best-known song by the band.

It sounds fantastic. Considering that it was recorded in a rehearsal space on a transplanted 8-track board, the depth and artistry of the production are remarkable. According to Kreiger, it was more or less composed on the spot, although it is likely that Morrison was drawing on material from his famous notebooks. Again, Jerry Scheff is critical here. The moment when Ray, Robby, and Jerry come together at the beginning of the song is a moment that never gets old. Robby's playing is off the scale throughout the song. His fills and responses to the vocal lines help to build the story. But it is also one of Ray's great moments as he textures each section with electric piano ideas. The slow section before Jim begins to chant 'Mr Mojo Risin'' is like a spacious jazz vignette. If Jim had returned from Paris in rude health, ready to lead The Doors to 1970s stadia glory, 'L.A. Woman' would have been a great barnstorming encore with plenty of room for improvisation.

Instead, it was played live only three times with Jim Morrison fronting the band. The Dallas version is worth hearing. It's a bit slower, a bit trippier, and still coming together.

The lyrics are evocative and clever. The city is at once a woman, perhaps Pamela Courson, and the place itself. 'I see your hair is burning / Hills are filled with fire' is both his red-headed muse and the city so often devastated by forest fires and, in Jim's time, riots. The song is filled with random images of the city – freeways, cops, topless bars. 'Motel, money, murder madness' could be an allusion to the Manson murders; an event foreshadowed in the darkness of The Doors' early music. Ray Manzarek sees the song as Jim's farewell to his adopted city. 'If they say I never loved you, you know they are a liar' echoes 'Light My Fire'. The phrase 'city of night' references, not for the first time in Morrison's lyrics, John Rechy's 1963 novel, *City Of Night*. His depiction of the LA demi-monde appealed strongly to Morrison and, interestingly, he returns to it on this album. The cinematic quality in his lyrics and the music, in general, is obvious here. It is almost like the beginning of a 1950s late noir film set in LA with a montage of urban scenes to set the stage for the story.

'Mr Mojo Risin'' is indeed an anagram of Jim Morrison. The scene has been set and the tension builds as Morrison chants about rising. A glorious song.

Side Two
'L'America' (The Doors)
I think it's fair to say that if this is the worst song on *L.A. Woman*, it would have been the best one on the *Zabriske Point* soundtrack. The film, *Zabriske Point*, is a dismal 1970 attempt by the Italian director Michelangelo Antonioni to cinematically render the counterculture. It has become a cult film in more recent years but is still a slog. The soundtrack includes fair to middling efforts by Pink Floyd, The Grateful Dead and The Youngbloods, but not The Doors.

Antonioni rejected 'L'America' when he heard it in 1969. A great cinema 'auteur' with questionable taste in music, perhaps.

In the wake of *Apocalypse Now*, filmmakers recognised the cinematic potential of this band, but in their time, surprisingly few directors came knocking. One might think that a band with not one but two graduates of a prestigious film school would have been an obvious choice to make soundtracks. In any case, one that did, knocked back this song.

It's intense and more psychedelic than anything else on the album and built around another memorable riff from The Doors. The first note sounds like the beginning of The Troggs' 'Wild Thing' but is followed by several more and some eerie wind-like sounds. With Ray adding triplets over the main riff, it builds in intensity until Jim starts singing. The next section is a blues rock bridge (C'mon people...), which is followed by a trippy section that resolves itself by wittily quoting The Rivieras garage punk classic 'California Sun'.

It's hard to imagine why Antonioni couldn't see the potential of this one. Like many Doors songs, it is inherently cinematic. It is also a good example of the postmodern quality of many of their best songs. It's a western, a border story, possibly even a sci-fi epic, all wrapped up in a garage punk mini-opera. One thing for sure, it is a lot more interesting than *Zabriske Point*!

It is not a well-known song, but it did provoke a reaction from John Fogerty, who said: 'The Doors always use those XYZ chords.' Listen to the song, and it becomes very clear what he means. It has not been widely covered though some have suggested that The Stranglers 'Sverige' bears a passing resemblance to it.

'Hyacinth House' (The Doors)

I'm always surprised to see this song dismissed as 'filler' on an otherwise great album. First of all, any 'classic' album is thus because there is some texture and shading with regard to the different tracks. Unless we're talking about The Ramones' first album, most great albums feature a range of songs that demonstrate the band's versatility and creative expanse. 'Hyacinth House' is a lovely song that, far from being filler, is a key component to *L.A. Woman*.

It was written a couple of years earlier at Robby's house. In fact, the song is about Robby's house that had hyacinths growing outside of the windows. According to Robby, the 'lions' mentioned in the first verse are a reference to his 'pet' bobcat. For some reason, he bought her as a kitten in a pet store and for a couple of years, she was cute and friendly. By the time Jim visited to write the song, she had begun to bite people and had to stay outside. He later gave her to a guy who collected wild cats, but the guy had had to shoot her when she attacked him. 'Poor kitty,' said Robby. 'But at least she is remembered in the song.'

John Densmore thinks it is Jim's saddest song. 'I need a brand new friend who doesn't need me' sounds to him like a cry for help. It is an uncharacteristically simple lyric for Jim and another hint that he might have had a future writing in the 1970s confessional mode as a solo artist or with The Doors. The odd line about the bathroom being free is supposedly just an observation he made after his friend Babe Hill returned to the living room.

Robby says in yet another of his guitar magazine interviews that it was recorded on a four-track at his place. The demo is well worth hearing and is available on *Box Set* and elsewhere. Considering that they have just written the song and that they were probably enjoying some recreational stimulants while observing a bobcat in the yard, it is a surprisingly good performance.

There is a lot of speculation about whether or not the use of 'Hyacinth' in the title is a veiled reference to the Greek myth of the beautiful young man killed accidentally by Apollo's discus. Jim was certainly interested in Greek mythology by way of Nietzsche, so this is entirely possible. This is yet another song that makes a brief reference to their first album with the final line: 'And I'll say it again, I need a brand new friend, the end'. While it isn't unusual for bands to look back at points in their career, it is worth remembering that The Doors had been together for only five years at this point.

'Crawling King Snake' (Hooker)

This is another track recorded on 'blues day', and one of three cover versions ever to appear on a Doors studio album; the other two are on their debut. It had been part of their repertoire since the London Fog days, and there are plenty of live versions available these days. You can hear an early version on the *Live At The Matrix* album, where you will find out very quickly why John Sebastian was asked to play harmonica on Roadhouse Blues! It was still on the setlist when the original quartet played their final show in New Orleans just before recording for this album commenced. In any case, it is clear from the performance on *L.A. Woman* that it was a song they knew very well and an arrangement that had been honed over the years. As far as their blues covers go, this may be one of the more successful. Morrison sings it with great flair. Robert Meltzer, in the original *Rolling Stone* review, says: 'And he's even a fair-to-middlin' blues gomper, because for the first time he honestly doesn't give a donut about how authentic or any of that the whole thing sounds.' I think that's a compliment.

The band probably knew John Lee Hooker's version best, but he was covering a little-known blues artist called Tony Hollins, who had recorded it in 1941, not long after Big Joe Williams' original release of the song in the same year. Snakes, for innuendo purposes, had long been part of the blues lexicon. Blind Lemon Jefferson's 1920s era 'Black Snake Moan' is an early example.

The Doors version features a variation of the blues riff that they had used previously on 'Maggie M'Gill'. John Lee Hooker's take might be the basis, but The Doors, by this point, had made this song their own. Ray is playing funky electric piano, and Robby releases his inner Alvin Lee on the guitar solo and at various other points in the song. Densmore says in his memoir that his drumming includes a fast roll tribute to Art Blakey, so, yes, this is The Doors using the song as a template rather than something to be faithfully reproduced.

It's not the highpoint of the record and, as the critic and Doors expert Richie Unterberger has pointed out, they weren't particularly exceptional interpreters of the blues. However, I think that it is an important part of the album because it grounds the other songs in Morrison's original concept of a blues outing.

There is also something wonderful about Jim finding an old song that combines his taste for innuendo with his enthusiasm for reptiles.

'WASP/Texas Radio And The Big Beat' (The Doors)

This is my favourite track on the album. From the opening chords to Morrison's spoken-word delivery, to Robby's guitar work after the 'for wasting the dawn' line, to John Densmore's incredible drumming, this is one of their finest and 'Doorsiest' moments. This is the Doors playing blues in a far more original and representative manner. It is also the source of one of Jim's most memorable lines: 'Out here we is stoned, immaculate.' Mic drop!

The poem had been part of their shows in 1968 as a lead up to 'Love Me Two Times'. There is a wonderful clip of this on Danish television. The television version is the one that first appeared on a 1980s live release called *Alive She Cried* and later on the *American Night* collection. On this recording, Morrison sounds a bit like Jack Kerouac in his delivery and the poem is certainly an excellent example of the Beat influence on his work. The words were printed in a 1968 tour booklet as well.

By the time they get to *L.A. Woman* several years later, the lyrics are the same, but now Morrison recites and sings the words over a blues riff in the spirit of the album. It's a powerful performance, and in a brilliant bit of song order, works perfectly as the light before the shade of 'Riders On The Storm'.

The Texas radio in question was, according to Manzarek, the border radio out of Del Rio, where Wolfman Jack and others played blues, rockabilly, and rock and roll that could be heard all the way to Canada on clear nights. Many artists of The Doors' generation from all over North America spent nights fine-tuning old radios to catch the powerful signal of these stations. In a sort of internet of sound, musicians like Robbie Robertson in Toronto, John Fogerty in San Francisco, Ray Manzarek in Chicago, and Jim Morrison in Florida were having their musical tastes shaped by the same sounds. The backbeat itself isn't hard to master. He is talking about the radio signal. If you ever tried to tune an old tube radio, you will know what he is getting at here.

The images are beautiful and mysterious, but there is a story here to do with music and escape. Huckleberry Finn's raft mingles with Exodus in the Old Testament here. Lines like 'live with us in forests of azure' and 'no eternal reward will forgive us now for wasting the dawn' are examples of Jim Morrison's extraordinary talent with language and verse. By this point in his career, he had been talking for several years about abandoning rock and roll for poetry. This was writing from a much earlier period, but his ability to perform spoken word is another sad reminder of what might have been for this gifted fellow.

'Riders On The Storm' (The Doors)

The final song on the final album with Jim. His whispered overdub, which can be heard at about the six-minute mark, is supposedly the last thing he ever recorded in a studio. The Doors, cinematic to the end, finished this stage of their career with one of the most memorable songs in rock and roll, an eerie tale that would have earned them a place in music history if it had been the only thing they'd ever recorded.

The story is that they were messing around with the old western standard 'Ghost Riders In The Sky', and somehow that evolved into 'Riders On The Storm'. The title itself is interesting. Some have attributed it to a line from 'Praise For An Urn', by Hart Crane, an American poet who Jim Morrison may have admired.

His thoughts, delivered to me
From the white coverlet and pillow,
I see now, were inheritances —
Delicate riders of the storm.

The poem was about a friend who had died in a car accident, and it is easy to see why Morrison would have been taken with it if indeed it was the source of the title. There is some evidence that Jim long believed he would die young and perhaps found something of value in this meditation on death. In any case, it is a highly evocative title for a song with deep philosophical underpinnings.

The opening verse of 'Riders On The Storm' repeats the title twice before introducing the following idea:

Into this house we're born
Into this world we're thrown

This is a concept identified with the German philosopher Martin Heidegger, who wrote about 'throwness', and the sense in which we all find ourselves in a particular context that is essentially arbitrary. Heidegger, a somewhat controversial figure today, is nonetheless one of the key philosophers of the 20th century. His ideas influenced the French existentialists, who in turn influenced both the American Beat writers and the New Wave in cinema. Jim Morrison reportedly attended lectures on Heidegger at Florida State University and would have undoubtedly come across him in his reading over the years.

Like a dog without a bone
Like an actor out on loan

The dog without access to something which will give meaning to its existence and the studio system actor rented out like an indentured slave are both images that underscore the Heideggerian concept of 'throwness'.

Morrison then tells the story of a hitchhiking serial killer. This is almost certainly based on the story of Billy Cook, who murdered several people, including an entire family while hitchhiking around the southwest and California in 1950. He was eventually caught and executed at San Quentin Prison. It was a famous story in the '50s, and it must have stuck with Morrison. A film that he made with friends in 1969 called *HWY* was inspired by it, to the extent that the main character is named Billy in the script. Scenes of Jim driving in this movie are commonplace in any Doors documentary and hundreds of YouTube clips. In the song, he combines Heidegger's idea with Billy's story by offering the listener the choice of whether or not to pick up the hitchhiker and outlining the dialectical implications of that choice.

There is also a long, complicated story about a road trip that Jim took in the early days of The Doors. It included a prank phone call about murdering one of his friends, that like so many Morrison stories, culminated in his arrest. There are so many versions of it that I can only suggest that you remember Colin Wilson's words on the possibility of vampires in medieval England – 'something happened!'

But 'Riders On The Storm' is more than simply a set of inspired lyrics. Robert Meltzer, in the original *Rolling Stone* review, makes the rather interesting comment that the song 'signalled the return to Del Shannon from whence The Doors' mysterioso-hood was largely derived, to begin with'. Assuming that he means Del's hit song Runaway, they do indeed share something of the minor mood and a dark atmosphere.

Thunder and rain, courtesy of Elektra's extensive sound effects library, get things started before Jerry Scheff's bass appears with Densmore's light percussion. The bass part was Manzarek's, who showed it to Scheff. Robby Kreiger has made the point that it is more melodic than what a bass player might have normally come up with, and Manzarek has mentioned that Scheff found it difficult to translate to bass guitar at first. His bass work on this album generally is wonderful, but it is nothing short of superb on this song.

But then everyone shines here. The Doors certainly had no idea that this would be their final statement with Jim Morrison, but they are playing as though they do. All of Manzarek's imaginative keyboard ability is on show here, and Robby's guitar work is outstanding. John Densmore shows once again that he can do so much more than simply keep time.

I suppose the tragedy here is that Jim Morrison sings this song so beautifully and with so much depth. This is not the last gasp of a croaky, washed-up former star delivering a substandard set of lyrics. If you didn't know better, you would conclude that you were listening to someone at the peak of their powers. In a sense, you would be correct.

The 45 of 'Riders On The Storm' reached 14 on the *Billboard* chart in July of 1971, just as the news of Jim's death was being reported. It remains a haunting reminder of his genius.

Other songs associated with L.A. Woman
'(You Need Meat) Don't Go No Further' (Dixon)

This Willie Dixon composition was recorded by Muddy Waters in the mid-fifties under the title 'Don't Go No Farther'. The Doors added the rather salacious bracketed bit to the title when they recorded it for this album. They also eschewed the earthy 'farther' for the more metaphysical 'further'. It was on the flip side of 'Love Her Madly' and appeared on the wonderful *Weird Scenes Inside The Goldmine* compilation in the early '70s. Ray Manzarek is the vocalist here. The fact is that Ray often covered for Jim on stage, particularly in the later years, so if he sounds a bit like the Lizard King, that's why. As The Doors' blues covers go, this is pretty standard fare but certainly worth hearing.

'Rock Me' (Waters)

You can read all about this song in the section on the London Fog recordings. This was another 'blues day' recording. It's a song that had figured in their live sets since their very earliest days, so they sound very comfortable here. Jim, in particular, is singing in a very natural way, somewhere in between blues shouter and Sinatra storyteller. It's not particularly revelatory, but since the song seems to have remained in their consciousness for so long, it is worth listening to and speculating on its appeal to the band.

'She Smells So Nice' (The Doors)

This is probably another 'blues day' entry. From the title to the 'blues by numbers' lyrics, this is more or less a jam. It's an up-tempo song in the 'Got My Mojo Working' mode, and an opportunity to hear the band in a slightly different gear. Ray's dexterity with this sort of music is on show here, and Jim is in good voice.

'Paris Blues' (The Doors)

A 'Holy Grail' track that has never been released and may have been partially erased. Ray Manzarek mentioned it once or twice in interviews, noting that it was a 'funky blues'. My guess is that it is another 'blues day' jam, perhaps best left to the imagination!

Other Voices (1971)

Recorded: June to August 1971 at Sunset Sound Recorders, Hollywood, California
Released: October 1971
Label: Elektra
Producer: Bruce Botnick and The Doors
Engineer: Bruce Botnick
Additional musicians: Jerry Scheff, Jack Conrad, Wolfgang Melz, Ray Neapolitan,
(bass guitar) Willie Ruff (acoustic bass), Francisco Aquabella (percussion)
Running Time: 39:42
Highest Chart Position: US:31 UK: did not chart

In Nick Coleman's fascinating book *Voices: How A singer Can Change Your Life*,
he suggests that we can be reasonably objective about instrumental music but
that there is something deeply personal about our response to human voices.
You can argue all day about whether Led Zeppelin is all about Jimmy Page's
guitar playing or Robert Plant's voice, but the fact is that you can probably still
listen to the band even if Page isn't entirely your cup of cider. It's a zero-sum
game with Plant. You like him or you don't. I know, objectively speaking, that
Rush are a great band, but, quite frankly, I can't listen to Geddy Lee. Voices are
the first sounds that we respond to emotionally as babies and it is very difficult
to step outside of our reaction to them.

Morrison's voice is one of the most distinctive sounds in rock and roll. There
is no mistaking him for someone else. Somehow, he could infuse even the
most banal line with dignity and depth. It didn't always make for stellar music,
of course, but throughout six studio albums, his strike rate was pretty good.
Without him, the band lost a key element in their sound. Even drunk or bored,
there was something about that voice that pulled things together. It seems
unfair to say Jim Morrison was The Doors, and it is demonstrably not true, but
somehow without him, nothing worked properly.

It wasn't only his voice but his presence. What is obvious when listening to
Other Voices and the follow-up, *Full Circle*, is that Jim was far more involved
in the overall sound and direction of the band than the many memoirs and
biographies would suggest. Despite the drinking, the arrests, missed shows
and recording dates, Jim Morrison was the leader of the band. He wasn't
particularly knowledgeable about music, but he knew what The Doors should
sound like. Without him, there is an obvious lack of focus. The playing on
this album is fine, excellent even. Some of the songs are pretty good. What's
missing is Jim's authority and vision.

In the early 1980s, you would often find *Other Voices* in The Doors section
at second-hand record shops. I remember being a bit confused about it when
I flipped it over and looked at the list of songs. None of them were on the
greatest hits album I owned or on *Weird Scenes Inside The Goldmine*. The
owner of the record store gently explained that this was a later album and
that if I already had all of The Doors' albums with Jim, I might want to try

something else instead. He went over to the rock section and returned with
Iggy And The Stooges' *Raw Power*. I loved it, of course, but I was always
curious about *Other Voices* and eventually bought a copy out of a bargain crate
a few years later. I played it once or twice and moved on.

The band was recording this album in July of 1971 when they got the news
that their singer had died in Paris. It's not entirely clear how much of the album
they had recorded and if they were simply treading water until Jim returned.
According to John Densmore, Jim phoned him not long before he died to ask
about the reaction to *L.A. Woman*. Densmore says that Jim was talking about
the future of the band and his role. If they seriously thought Jim Morrison
was coming back, they must not have been too far along with this album. This
raises an obvious point. Jim died in July and the album appeared in October. It
was done quickly and in the shadow of a tragedy. When it appeared, 'Riders On
The Storm' was still in the charts. What was the rush?

My sense is a mixture of panic and trauma. Whatever had developed between
Jim and the remaining three members of the band, he had loomed large in
their lives. The demise of Jim Morrison now seems inevitable. He had problems
with alcohol, exhibited self-destructive behaviour, and sang gloomy songs
about death. But that could describe any number of rockers who are still
making music today. At the time, Morrison's death was a terrible shock to those
who knew him. In a movie, this album would have been a tribute to a fallen
soldier, a dark masterpiece. The reality is an uneven album by a band that has
lost the element by which they were best known. In retrospect, one wonders
why they didn't wait a year or two, but they didn't, so we have *Other Voices*.

Side One
'In The Eye Of The Storm' (Manzarek)
This is a cool song that one could easily imagine Jim singing on another 'blues
day'. It's not miles away from their Elektra label mate, Tim Buckley's moves
into a funkier zone. Ray's limitations as a singer are on show here, but the
band is tight. They sound like The Doors as Robby digs out the slide and Ray
finds a groove on keyboards, but perhaps more like a band imitating The Doors
than the real thing.

'Variety Is The Spice Of Life' (Kreiger)
One of the many anomalies about The Doors is that despite the towering figure
of Jim Morrison, poet, shaman, etc., it was Robby Kreiger who wrote almost
all of the hits. Logically, Robby's post Morrison work should be in the vein of
'Light My Fire' or 'Love Her Madly', songs that the listener can easily conjure
up Jim singing. This is, sadly, not the case here. While not a terrible song, it is a
departure from the band's previous work. First of all, it seems to be some sort
of a homage to occasional Doors harmonica man, John Sebastian's 'Did You
Ever Have To Make Up Your Mind?' Robby's singing is probably more serviceable
than Ray's but doesn't have enough character to bring this song to life.

'Ships With Sails' (Kreiger, Densmore)

This is the best song on the album and the one that comes closest to fulfilling the promise of a Doors album. The opening, featuring guest Francisco Aquabella's percussion and Robby's guitar playing, is glorious. The vocals are shared by Robby and Ray, and they sound pretty good here. It evolves into a funky jam over a Latin rhythm, and after the disappointment of 'Variety is the Spice of Life', I'm sure the original listener thought that they had their band back. It's a shame that the band didn't head in the direction of this song. The influence of the Grateful Dead seems obvious here and it isn't a bad fit at all. The Dead's vocals have never been their most notable feature. Groove, extended jams, and soundscapes were The Dead's real signature. The Doors could do all three with great flair. Without Jim, it would have made sense to change the focus of things and head in a more progressive direction. 'Ships with Sails' would have been a good start. Needless to say, Jim would have knocked this one out of the park.

'Tightrope Ride' (Manzarek, Kreiger)

Ray Manzarek decides that it is time to party like it's 1965 on this one. This three chord garage scorcher was the first single from this album and, if not for the freight of The Doors career, would be an obvious choice for Nuggets style collections. It kicks off with a classic solo electric guitar measure before Ray lets loose on the organ and launches into the sub-Dylan accusatory lyrics. Some people think that the mention of Brian Jones is a coded reference to Jim and that this was written for the singer. I suspect this was written well before Jim died. I suspect that this was written in exactly the year it sounds like it was written in, 1965. It's a lot closer to the Rick & The Ravens singles than anything by The Doors, and sounds as though it was cooked up after hearing Dylan's 'Like A Rolling Stone' come blasting out of the radio that year. In any case, it's a lively song with a stunning Jerry Scheff bass line.

Side Two

'Down On The Farm' (Kreiger)

If 'Tightrope Ride' sounds like 1965, this is 1968. It's psychedelic, with a touch of cosmic country. Another of Robby's songs, this is essentially a 'getting it together in the country' idea with two distinct sections. He sings well in a Bob Weir-esque sort of way, and the band is more than capable of building an appropriate backdrop. There is a moment where someone is playing a harmonica in the wrong key, badly, which makes it sound like an outtake, but otherwise, this is okay.

'I'm Horny, I'm Stoned' (Kreiger)

I don't think Jim Morrison would have sung this one. It's another of Robby's compositions, and sounds vaguely like a lost San Francisco psychedelic nugget from a slightly earlier period. The ludicrous title aside, it's not a terrible song. A bit of an earworm even...

'Wandering Musician' (Kreiger)
This is another Ray Manzarek song. It's a ballad with some nifty changes and nice guitar work from Robby. Again, Ray sings with passion, but he just doesn't have the chops. It would have been interesting to hear this one with a better singer. The chorus has a John Lennon feel and it is easy to imagine it working well live.

'Hang On To Yourself' (Manzarek, Kreiger)
This opens with a cooking rhythm, courtesy of Francisco Aquabella. Ray and Robby jam away before Ray begins to sing. Somewhere in the middle, the tempo picks up for a jammy freak out with some great bass work from the interesting figure of Wolfgang Melz. Again, The Dead seemed to be an influence, but the whole thing seems a bit dated. That said, it's worth hearing, and I like to ignore the singing and imagine that it is part of the proggy instrumental album they should have done at this stage. As Robert Christgau said of this record, 'this band needs a singer'.

Full Circle (1972)

Recorded: April to June 1972 at A&M Studios, Hollywood, CA
Released: August 1972
Label: Elektra
Producer: The Doors
Engineer: Henry Lewy
Additional musicians: Jack Conrad, Leland Sklar, Chris Etheridge, Charles Larkey
(bass guitar) Charles Lloyd (tenor saxophone, flute) Chico Batera, Bobbeye Hall
(percussion) Veneta Fields, Clydie King, Melissa Mackay (vocals)
Running Time: 40:05
Highest Chart Position: US: 68 UK: did not chart

This was it for our heroes. Within a year of the release of *Full Circle*, it was all
over. There would be *An American Prayer* in 1978, which is covered in this
book, some solo records, a few one-off reunions, something called The Doors
of the 21st Century, and, for Robby Kreiger, a million or so interviews in guitar
magazines. But for the band that had begun with a conversation on Venice
Beach in the summer of 1965, this was the last album as a working outfit.

It is also the second album without Jim and perhaps the only real indication
of what a Morrison-less Doors might have sounded like. *Other Voices*, as I have
noted, is the sound of a band in shock. *Full Circle*, despite its shortcomings,
sounds more like what one might have expected from the remaining members.

It was recorded at A&M Studios in Hollywood. Bruce Botnick decided that
his time with The Doors was up and turned over the engineering duties to
Henry Lewy, who had worked with Joni Mitchell and Neil Young, among
others. The Doors themselves are listed as producers. I suppose one might
wonder what would have happened if Paul Rothchild had come back, but it
was not to be.

I was going to say that one of the obvious points to be made about *Full Circle*
is that the songs fall into one of two camps. There are the 'maybe this will be
a hit single' songs like 'Get Up and Dance' and there are the moody long-form
jams like 'Verdilac'. It occurred to me, however, that all of The Doors albums,
with the possible exception of *Morrison Hotel*, featured a range of potential
pop hits mixed in with more experimental fare. It could be argued that The
Doors never fully embraced the idea of the 'album' in its full post Pepper
sense. On some level, they were always a mid-sixties garage band hoping for a
top ten hit. At points on *Full Circle,* you can hear the bones of what might have
been a great jazz rock concept album. At other points, you hear a trite set of
lyrics, a forgettable melody, and a dull arrangement being run up the flag pole
in the desperate hope that someone might salute.

The standard critical line is that *Other Voices* is okay-ish, and *Full Circle* is
a train wreck. Don't believe it. *Full Circle* is a far better record than *Other
Voices*. It is not a masterpiece, and it is not on par with any of the Morrison
era records, but it is not terrible. It has some real highlights and at least one

stellar track that finally delivers on the Jazz influence often claimed by various members of the band.

However, it does, like *Other Voices*, give some insight into the role of Jim Morrison. In his guide to albums of the 1970s, Robert Christgau's review takes the form of a single question: 'Is this slick eclecticism what all those experts who used to claim Jim Morrison was limiting his musicians had in mind?' In other words, the sense that Jim Morrison was somehow the problem in the band bears scrutiny. Whatever role he might have taken in the day to day operations, he represented a creative centre. Perhaps it was that he maintained a relationship with all of the members and, even while he was being arrested or late for a recording session, was a point of contact, a crucial part of the social dynamic that made The Doors. If The Beatles couldn't survive Yoko turning up to recording sessions, how were The Doors ever going to go on without Jim Morrison? With that gloomy question in mind, we will put on big Ray Manzarek smiles and listen to what might be the least known album by a major band.

Side One
'Get Up And Dance' (Manzarek, Kreiger)
I will come right out and say it: this is the worst track on the album. It was the first single and features female backup singers, including Clydie King, who sang on Sweet Home Alabama and a stack of Dylan albums. It is the very definition of early '70s 'mellow' rock. It is also a very boring song that sounds like someone imitating Delaney and Bonnie. True, it features former Flying Burrito Chris Etheridge playing bass very nicely, and the girls do help with the vocals (an old trick), but it seems to say nothing and go nowhere in a very un-Doors like manner.

'4 Billion Souls' (Kreiger)
This is no masterpiece either, but at least it sounds like The Doors. In a pinch, the listener can almost imagine Morrison giving the vapid lyrics some much-needed gravitas in his delivery. At this stage, Robby had left off the continuing saga of his marriage to Lynn and begun to write rather vague lyrics about 'people' and 'the world'. When 'best' is rhymed with 'rest' in a short song, I start looking at my watch. That said, it features some interesting chord changes and nifty bass work from Jack Conrad, who would tour with them after the album's release.

'Verdilac' (Manzarek, Kreiger)
This is where things get very interesting on *Full Circle*. The wonderful jazz woodwind player, Charles Lloyd joins them on tenor sax here and things heat up. He is a natural fit. One of the only nice things Jim could say about *The Soft Parade* album was that 'Touch Me' featured the first jazz saxophone solo in a pop song. 'Verdilac' delivers on that long-ago promise. Ray, Robbie and John

97

had long been threatening a jazz rock turn, and they finally got to work here. Robby, in particular, goes head to head with the formidable Lloyd and holds his own. If you only listen to one track from this record, try this one. There are unnecessary vocals, but they disappear quickly. Every time I listen to this album, I hear this song and wish that they had gone the whole hog and done a 22-minute version as the first half of the album and left the other four songs on side one in the can.

'Hardwood Floor' (Kreiger)

You just wish someone, Paul Rothchild maybe, had dropped by and, after listening to this one, said, 'You are not Poco, you are The Doors for heaven's sake.' Some agreeable keyboarding from Ray, a serviceable harmonica part by Robby, but otherwise just a predictable set of lyrics in a bland country rock setting.

'Good Rockin' (Brown)

This old Roy Brown warhorse always gets a thrashing from critics writing about this album. It was the flipside of their final single, 'The Piano Bird', and is generally described as filler. I think it's a decent rockabilly workout from a band who could handle it. It's more or less in the tradition of their Morrison era blues covers and it would have been interesting to have heard him on this one. That said, Ray's vocal performance is pretty good. Jack Conrad's capable bass playing lifts things considerably as well.

Side Two
'The Mosquito' (Manzarek, Kreiger, Densmore)

If you've never heard this one, you might need to listen to it before reading any further. The first minute is, shall we say, unexpected. The jam that follows is a funky groove with some serious guitar pyrotechnics from Robby, who wrote the song. But that first section with Spanish lines about the mosquito and the burrito is possibly the oddest entry in their entire catalogue. It was released as a single in the fall of 1972 and reached the lower rungs of the *Billboard* chart. Robby claims that it was their biggest selling post-Jim single because it 'was in Spanish' and did well all over the world. It's a little difficult to believe that the line 'No me moleste mosquito / Let me eat my burrito' endeared it to Spanish speaking listeners, but I guess he knows how many sold.

'The Piano Bird' (Conrad, Densmore)

This was the final single from the album and is another strong track featuring Charles Lloyd, this time on flute. He played with them on a couple of live dates in the US and has said that he enjoyed working with the band. With two outstanding percussionists, Chico Batera and Bobbye Hall, along with Jack Conrad on bass, this works well. Again, the lyrics leave something to be desired, and the singing is still a problem, but this is still a very listenable slice of jazz rock. If only they'd dropped the lame attempts at country rock and stuck to this sort of thing, there really might have been a second act.

'It Slipped My Mind' (Kreiger)

Except for the bland vocals, this could be an outtake from *Waiting For The Sun*. It was the flipside of Mosquito and would have certainly reminded listeners that they were listening to The Doors. It isn't particularly memorable, but Robby's guitar solo and the sound of the band doing their thing makes it worth a listen or two.

'The Peking King And The New York Queen' (Manzarek, Kreiger)

I'm sorry, but this is dreadful. It is boring instrumentally, badly sung, and features lyrics that are both ridiculous and pretentious. It is some sort of overwrought metaphor to do with Nixon's visit to China. I try not to think about the fact that this is the last song on their final album.

Other songs associated with *Full Circle*
'Tree Trunk' (Kreiger)

This was the B-side of 'Get Up And Dance' and is arguably a better song. It was written by Robby and is another of his post-Jim, country rock, *Workingman's Dead* style songs. This one is a variation on the Hollies' 'Bus Stop' idea with an old tree trunk instead of an umbrella.

An American Prayer (1978)

Recorded: 1969 at Elektra Sound Studios, 1970 at Village Sound Studios (Jim
Morrison's spoken word recordings). 1978 at Hollywood Sound Recorders (new
material)
Released: November 1978
Label: Elektra/Asylum
Producer: John Haeny, The Doors, Paul Rothchild, Bruce Botnick
Additional musicians: Jerry Scheff, Bob Glaub (bass guitar)
Running Time: 38:28
Highest Chart Position: US: 54, UK: did not chart

What is this exactly? Some might say that it was an attempt to cash in on The
Doors' popularity with some old spoken word material that Morrison recorded
in '69 and '70. Sure, why not? The Doors had been Elektra's hottest property
until Jim had gone and died in Paris. This material was available, and the
remaining members of the band needed the work. It sounds possible, but the
problem with the story is that, believe it or not, there was a time when The
Doors were a slightly mouldy old band from the '60s. If this album had been
released after Jim Morrison ended up on the cover of *Rolling Stone* in 1981
with the memorable tag line, 'He's hot, he's sexy, and he's dead,' then *An
American Prayer* would indeed seem like an example of scraping the bottom
of the barrel to squeeze every last dollar out of a once again lucrative franchise.
But that's not what happened.

This album was, at least on one level, a form of closure for the band and
John Haeny, who made the original recordings of much of this material. Jim
Morrison was going to make a spoken word record but died before it got past
the initial steps. At two sessions, more than a year apart, he recorded what are
essentially rehearsal tapes or demos. This might seem like his record company
indulging their star's ego with no intention whatsoever to go ahead, but this
is Elektra in the 1960s and, amazingly, there was a contract drawn up for this
album. What it was to be called or how it would have turned out, we will never
know. What we have instead is *An American Prayer*, a record that, for all its
faults, remains a fascinating listening experience. If you have just listened to
the two post-Jim albums, there is something magic about hearing Jim's voice
again. He is reciting poetry, but he always did sound like an 'actor out on loan'
(sorry, irresistible!), even when he was singing.

Paul Rothchild hates this record and considers it a desecration of Jim's
memory. He says that Jim did not want the other Doors involved and had
approached Lalo Schifrin to do the music. Who knows? John Haeny, who is
credited as a producer here, made the call to include both original Doors
music from their albums and new recordings by Kreiger, Manzarek, and
Densmore. Should he have called Lalo instead? I don't think so.

What this isn't is what appears on *The Lost Paris Tapes* album. That is an
edited version of the session Jim did at Elektra Sound Studios in February of

1969, based on a tape that Haeny gave Jim to take to Paris. *An American Prayer* is a mix of Jim Morrison's spoken word material from a range of sources, including the 1969 session, the 1970 session at Village Sound, the production tape of Morrison's film *HWY*, a recording made of Jim talking in a Palm Springs motel room, live recordings from Doors concerts, edited sections of album tracks, and new material by the remaining band members. It is not, perhaps, what Jim had in mind, but functions as a sound documentary and a tribute to his obvious talent as a poet.

An American Prayer is, above all, a better way to end things than *Full Circle*. The remaining Doors, Ray, in particular, saw it as a way to honour Jim's intention to be a poet. For John Haeny, it was perhaps a means to deliver on a promise made to Jim. For the rest of us, it was some new material from a band whose career had been pretty short. This isn't everybody's cup of coffee, but I like it.

Side One
'Awake' (Morrison, The Doors)
The album opens with the 'Is everybody in?' section of 'The Celebration Of The Lizard', recorded live. Jim's delivery is powerful, and the audience response is ecstatic. It's a reminder that even at the height of their popularity, Jim Morrison was performing poetry on stage and pushing the boundaries of what constituted a rock and roll show.

'Ghost Song' (Morrison, The Doors)
Morrison recorded this at Village Studios in the second session with John Haeny, and the remaining Doors recorded a musical backdrop in 1978. It's interesting to hear the band as it stands more than five years after their final show. The music is jazz-oriented and very much of its time, but it is still The Doors. Manzarek's raindrop piano notes sound as Jim begins the story. Robby's guitar work is punctuated by Jerry Scheff's funky bass lines. The poem takes the listener to sea, a frequent Morrison setting, and a Dionysian scene of dancing and laughing. It's not hard to imagine an alternative 1978 where Jim is recording something like this with the band.

'Dawn's Highway' (Morrison, The Doors)
After the 'Indians scattered on dawn's highway' couplet from 'Peace Frog', we hear Jim in conversation telling the famous story of a car accident he witnessed as a child. This was drawn from what is known as *The Endless Night Tapes*, which are recordings made of Jim talking, telling stories, and reciting poetry in a Palm Springs motel room. Part of John Haeny and the remaining Doors' intentions was to demonstrate the relationship between Jim's storytelling, his poetry and his songwriting. They felt like this recording of him telling the story that would eventually make its way into 'Peace Frog' needed to be on the album. The problem was that Jim was almost drowned out on the tape

101

by a cheap motel air conditioning unit. John Haeny took the tape to a man called Thomas Stockham, who had famously restored Enrico Caruso's early recordings using a system called 'blind de-convolution', an early digital process that allowed him to separate Jim from the air conditioning. The results are, for the time, remarkable. Haeny added the sound of wind to create an incredibly eerie moment on the album.

'Newborn Awakening' (Morrison, The Doors)
The motel room recording gives way to the section in 'Peace Frog' where he tells the story. As the song drifts into 'Blue Sunday', we hear Jim's voice reciting the 'Indian, Indian' couplet. The next section, to my ears, does not sound like Jim reading, but it may be that his voice has been manipulated. In any case, the poem is evocative and spooky. He alludes to the Ghost Dance, the nineteenth-century Native American practice, and integrates his Nietzschean sense of a new age with Native imagery.

'To Come Of Age' (Morrison, The Doors)
This track begins with the execution sequence from 'The Unknown Soldier', before giving way to what sounds like Jim's 1967 Mustang taking off. 'A military station in the desert,' says Jim, who knew something about these places from childhood. He refers to coming of age in a dry place, and the words seem to be fragments of adolescent memories.

'Black Polished Chrome' (Morrison, The Doors)
This sequence, along with 'To Come Of Age', is drawn from a cycle called 'Tales From The American Night', which was recorded at the first session with John Haeny in 1969. It tells the story of a DJ coming to his school and playing music for a dance. It seems to be related to the 'The WASP', as a memory of hearing 1950s rock and roll and rhythm and blues as a teenager. The Doors provide a recording of suitable kick-ass blues grooves. Robby sounds great here.

'Latino Chrome' (Morrison, The Doors)
'My gang will get you,' says Jim, as the Doors kick into a slinky Latin jazz backing track. This cinematic set of images evokes a sleazy version of urban life before giving way to what sounds like a sermon of some kind.

'Angels And Sailors' (Morrison, The Doors)
This is one of the more fully realised pieces here, though it is not for the faint of heart. It is the story of a sailor with two girls in his hotel room, and Morrison doesn't hold back with the more salacious details. At the end, he says, famously, 'we could plan a murder or start a religion'. During this story, there is a section of 'I Will Never Be Untrue', a lovely country blues recorded both in the 'Rock is Dead' session and for *Morrison Hotel*.

'Stoned Immaculate' (Morrison, The Doors)
The point here seems to be to show how the spoken word section in 'The WASP' evolved from Jim's poetry. Sections of the song are mashed up with edits from the 1969 session with John Haeny.

'The Movie' (Morrison, The Doors)
'Did you have a good world, enough to base a movie on?' This is an intriguing track drawn again from the first poetry recordings in 1969. Again, it demonstrates Morrison's talents as a performance poet. Considering his interest in film and the cinematic quality of his lyrics, his notion of life as a movie works well. The answer to the question in Jim's case is, somewhat regrettably, yes.

'Curses, Invocations' (Morrison, The Doors)
This is another track that one could easily imagine appearing on a notional later Doors record had Jim lived. The band's groove fits perfectly with his carnivalesque images. 'I'll always be a word man, better than a birdman,' says Jim to finish this small gem.

'American Night' (Morrison, The Doors)
This brief section provides a dramatic introduction to 'Roadhouse Blues'. Again, the idea seems to be linking Jim's poetic concepts – the American night in this case – to his lyrics. 'Roadhouse Blues', like many Doors songs, is set in a night world, so the juxtaposition highlights his noir-ish imagination.

'Roadhouse Blues' (Morrison, The Doors)
A rocking splice of two versions from the 1970 tour, and Jim's views on astrology. According to John Haeny, the original idea was to use a recording of The Doors' version of 'Gloria' from the Aquarius Theatre soundcheck. This did not sit well with Pamela Courson's father, Corky, who felt that the song, or at least Morrison's rendering of it, was sexist. Haeny doesn't give any further details about his objection other than making it clear that he did not argue and began to search for a replacement. Corky Courson shared the rights to all of this material at the time.

Side Two
'The World on Fire' (Morrison, The Doors)
Against the fading crowd noises, a brief set of lines from the Village sessions of 1970. I like the idea of a 'taxi from Africa'.

'Lament' (Morrison, The Doors)
This is, on one level, cringeworthy. However, considering the trouble that Jim's, ahem, member, had caused, these lines are also hilarious. Whatever the case, his ability with imagery is on show in this Beat influenced piece.

'The Hitchhiker' (Morrison, The Doors)
The story that underpins 'Riders On The Storm', a murderous hitch-hiker, is also a component of Jim's film *HWY*. The phone call in this piece, apparently to the poet Michael McClure, is the fictitious (hopefully) story of a murder. 'Riders On The Storm' plays quietly under Jim's voice. This story seems to go back to an actual event where Jim claimed to have murdered a friend he had bickered with on a road trip and ended up in jail on an unrelated charge. Whatever the inspiration, the image of a lone killer hitchhiking in the desert seems to have resonated with Morrison.

'An American Prayer' (Morrison, The Doors)
This is a fully realised piece, matched with new music from the band. It is from the Village sessions of 1970 and is, as advertised, a long-form profane prayer. It is a fitting finale to the record, as Morrison calls for a reinvention of the gods and myths and something like a Dionysian revolution. The music is the same jam used for 'Ghost Song', but works even better here.

'Hour For Magic' (Morrison, The Doors)
A coda to the prayer over the freak out instrumental section of 'The End'. Lovely.

'Freedom Exists' (Morrison, The Doors)
A brief Beat-style protest poem.

'A Feast Of Friends' (Morrison, The Doors)
A lovely and sad finish to an album that highlights the extraordinary talents of someone who died far too young. The Doors play Albioni's 'Adagio in G Minor' as Jim recites these mysterious lines that betray a prophetic weariness with the world.

Extra Tracks
'Babylon Fading' (Morrison, The Doors)
A strange brief piece that makes liberal use of sound effects.

'Bird of Prey' (Morrison)
Lovely lyrics sung a-cappella by Jim from the 1969 sessions.

Live Albums

As I noted earlier, live rock and roll albums are a pretty mixed bag. If the goal is to put the listener somewhere in the first few rows, this is rarely achieved. There are some wonderful exceptions, but the pure sensory experience of a rock and roll show, particularly in the old days before safe plastic glasses of champagne and ushers, is hard to capture. The Doors were, by all accounts, a thrilling live act. Morrison was an actor, an acrobat, a comedian, a preacher, a poet, a politician, and a very capable singer. His influences were Beat poets, Dionysian shamans, and, disastrously at least once, revolutionary theatre directors. The band behind him were rock-solid players who loved to improvise and follow Jim wherever the journey took him. He wasn't always at his best, but when he was, he reinvented the role of lead singer and set a standard for performance that few have equalled.

The first point is that there are a lot of live albums available. Since 2000, Rhino has been releasing complete shows and compilations with the assistance of Doors engineer and producer Bruce Botnick at the Bright Midnight Archive. Some of these might not appear regularly at your local music shop, but they can be obtained in some format or another. Some are also pretty expensive, so unless you are a completist, you will want to spend some time listening to the tracks available online before you start buying. Many of them are from the 1970 tour, so there is considerable overlap in the setlists. There are also, of course, bootlegs floating around, despite the waterfall of official releases. There are recordings of several European shows that are worth tracking down that have yet to be given the Bright Midnight treatment. Below I have noted most of the Bright Midnight releases and commented briefly on them.

I have covered *Absolutely Live* already, and that was the only live record released while the band was together. The following three albums appeared in the wake of the revival of interest in the band in the early 1980s and the success of the 1980 *Greatest Hits* record.

Alive She Cried (1983) features material from three shows later released in their entirety, Aquarius Theatre 1969, New York 1970, Boston 1970, as well as two tracks recorded for television in Denmark. I remember being a bit underwhelmed by it at the time.

Hollywood Bowl (1987) is the sound recording of a filmed concert from 1968. Because so much of the available live material is from later tours, it's worth hearing this one. It was re-released in 2012 as *Live At The Bowl*. Highlight: 'Wake Up'. Jim is on fire here.

In Concert (1991) is essentially a compilation of the previous three live albums.

Rhino/Bright Midnight Archives Releases:

Live In Detroit (2000) is a recording of a 1970 show at the Cobo Theatre in Detroit. This is The Doors in blues mode, with John Sebastian joining in on harmonica for a few songs. Highlight: 'Been Down So Long' – John Sebastian should have been on the recorded version.

Live At The Aquarius Theatre (2001) (first and second performances), and *Live in Hollywood* (2002), are a series of albums that chronicle several Hollywood shows by the band in July of 1969. At the moment, they seem to be only available for download. These shows were one of the sources for *Absolutely Live* and *Alive She Cried,* so the sound quality is pretty good on all three. Highlight: the instrumental 'Peace Frog' on the second performance, but you'll no doubt find your own highlight if you work your way through this document of a band at the height of their powers.

Backstage And Dangerous (2002) is a rehearsal tape from backstage at the Aquarius Theatre on the second day of their stop in Hollywood. The story is that Paul Rothchild wanted them to be sharp for the next performance, as it was being recorded for a live release that would eventually morph into the pastiche that is *Absolutely Live.* This is something mainly for hardcore fans, but it is interesting to hear them working up things like 'Gloria' and 'Mystery Train'. It's a peek behind the curtains, but not something you would put on for easy listening. Highlight: a lovely version of 'I Will Never Be Untrue', a song mysteriously absent from their recorded output.

Boot Yer Butt (2003): appalling sound quality, but some interesting bits and pieces from shows that weren't professionally recorded. Richie Unterberger says it's for fans, if not scholars only. Highlight: this is a tough listen, but it is interesting to hear a live version of 'Who Scared You?'

Live In Philadelphia (2005) is another download-only recording of a 1970 show. The sound quality is okay, and as this is in the same week as the Detroit show, the blues mood is here too. No obvious highlights, but I like the loose version of 'Ship Of Fools'.

Live In Boston (2007) is another 1970 tour date consisting of two shows rendered in full. It's an interesting glimpse of a concert where Jim is a little drunk but in an expansive mood. What I mean is that there is a lot of chit chat, poetry, and improvisation here. There were a lot of good shows musically on the tour, and you can listen to most of them, but this was a different sort of evening. Highlight: 'Away In India' jam from the first show. Cool.

Live In Pittsburgh (2008) is, yes, the night after Philly on the 1970 tour. Jim is in much better form here and the band sounds tighter. This is well worth tracking down. Highlight: 'Someday Soon', a great lost Doors track.

Live At The Matrix (2008) is among the earliest available recordings of the band. This is from a series of shows at The Matrix club in San Francisco, just after the first album had been released and well before they had a number one hit with 'Light My Fire'. Bootlegs of these shows have been available for years, but the sound quality is much better on this official release. I love this album because it's The Doors when they were still a Hollywood garage band. The contrast with something like *Live in Boston* is remarkable considering that there are only three years between them. Jim is still finding his voice and his stage presence, but there is a freshness and hunger in his performances. Highlight: 'Summer's Almost Gone'.

Live In New York (2009) is a multi-CD set of the shows that The Doors played at the Felt Forum in January of 1970. This might be the one to track down if you are interested in any of the Bright Midnight Material. To my ears, the sound quality is excellent, and the band are in good form. John Sebastian turned up for the encore of the final show but had to rerecord his parts decades later because his mic wasn't being recorded by the mobile unit. He still sounds great on 'Rock Me'. Highlight: a top version of 'Universal Mind', but, again, you'll soon find your favourites here.

Live In Vancouver (2010) is a recording of another 1970 show, but one that features none other than Albert King on several songs. Otherwise, it's another blues-oriented date. Jim says nice things about Vancouver and seems to enjoy playing with Albert. Highlight: 'Little Red Rooster'.

Live At The Isle Of Wight (2018) also took place in August of 1970 but has a different mood than most of the other shows from the tour. It was filmed and you can watch it on YouTube. Ray Manzarek felt that Jim was in a sombre state, almost as though he was deliberately shutting down everything except his voice. No real highlights, though the long medley beginning with 'The End' is engaging. The footage is fascinating. It is worth noting that The Doors only played two more dates with Jim after this concert. In December 1970, they played two shows in Dallas and a final one in New Orleans. While there are recordings available of individual songs from these shows, the sound quality is poor, so this is the best place to hear The Doors at the end.

Collections, Greatest Hits, Box Sets, and Weird Scenes Inside The Goldmine

If you have somehow decided, after reading this book, that a mere compilation will suffice, there are plenty of them out there. In 1980, in the wake of *Apocalypse Now*, and growing interest in the band, the *Greatest Hits* album with a red-hued picture of Jim on the cover was released. If you are in your fifties, you will recall that everyone you knew owned it. I can remember realising that I somehow had two cassette copies, neither of which I could remember buying. Nowadays, the 2017 collection, *The Doors: The Singles*, is probably a better place to start. It includes 'Mosquito' from *Full Circle*. You've been warned!

If you want to dig deep, there are a couple of rarities collections out there and, if you can find it at a reasonable price, the 1997 box set is something to snap up. It has all kinds of gems, both from the studio and live, including the 1965 demo recordings. It includes 'Orange County Suite', a lovely song that Jim sang and accompanied on piano during the first spoken word session in 1969. The remaining Doors added backing here. You can hear the original version on the 40th-anniversary edition of *L.A. Woman*. It's a gem.

I will finish with the magnificent *Weird Scenes Inside The Goldmine*, a double album that was released in 1973 but given to me by my mum as a slightly ill-advised 14th birthday present in 1980. I have no idea how the songs were chosen, but the overall impression that it made on me was that The Doors were an appealingly dark and vaguely experimental act. It's a mix of singles, B-sides and 'deep cuts' that live up to the name and creepy album art. It seems to be available again on LP, and I recommend it highly, particularly if you are trying to interest a teenage relative in this wonderful band.

Further Reading

There are a lot of books about Jim Morrison and The Doors. I found the following useful:

Jim Cherry, *The Doors Examined* (Bennion Kearny Ltd 2013)
Stephen Davis, *Jim Morrison: Life, Death, Legend* (Gotham 2004)
John Densmore, *Riders On The Storm* (Arrow Books, 1991)
Ray Manzarek, *Light My Fire* (Berkley 1999)
Greil Marcus, *The Doors: A Lifetime Of Listening To Five Mean Years* (Public Affairs 2011)
James Riordan, *Break On Through: The Life And Death Of Jim Morrison* (It Books, 1991)
Mick Wall, *Love Becomes A Funeral Pyre: A Biography Of The Doors* (Chicago Review Press 2015)
Rick Weidman, *The Doors FAQ: All That's Left To Know About The Kings of Acid Rock* (Backbeat Books 2011)

And, with a grain of salt, it is still a cracking read:
No One Here Gets Out Alive, Jerry Hopkins and Danny Sugerman (Plexus 1980)

Other related books
Barney Hoskyns, *Waiting For The Sun: Strange Days, Weird Scenes, And The Sound Of Los Angeles* (Penguin 1996)
Dominic Priore, *Riot On Sunset Strip: Rock And Roll's Last Stand In 60s Hollywood* (Jawbone 2007)

Websites
There is no shortage of Doors material online, but I found these two websites very helpful:
www.doorshistory.com/
http://mildequator.com/

Also available from Sonicbond

On Track series
Tori Amos – Lisa Torem 978-1-78952-142-9
Asia – Peter Braidis 978-1-78952-099-6
Barclay James Harvest – Keith and Monica Domone 978-1-78952-067-5
The Beatles – Andrew Wild 978-1-78952-009-5
The Beatles Solo 1969-1980 – Andrew Wild 978-1-78952-030-9
Blue Oyster Cult – Jacob Holm-Lupo 978-1-78952-007-1
Marc Bolan and T.Rex – Peter Gallagher 978-1-78952-124-5
Kate Bush – Bill Thomas 978-1-78952-097-2
Camel – Hamish Kuzminski 978-1-78952-040-8
Caravan – Andy Boot 978-1-78952-127-6
Eric Clapton Solo – Andrew Wild 978-1-78952-141-2
The Clash – Nick Assirati 978-1-78952-077-4
Crosby, Stills and Nash – Andrew Wild 978-1-78952-039-2
The Damned – Morgan Brown 978-1-78952-136-8
Deep Purple and Rainbow 1968-79 – Steve Pilkington 978-1-78952-002-6
Dire Straits – Andrew Wild 978-1-78952-044-6
The Doors – Tony Thompson 978-1-78952-137-5
Dream Theater – Jordan Blum 978-1-78952-050-7
Elvis Costello and The Attractions – Georg Purvis 978-1-78952-129-0
Emerson Lake and Palmer – Mike Goode 978-1-78952-000-2
Fairport Convention – Kevan Furbank 978-1-78952-051-4
Peter Gabriel – Graeme Scarfe 978-1-78952-138-2
Genesis – Stuart MacFarlane 978-1-78952-005-7
Gentle Giant – Gary Steel 978-1-78952-058-3
Gong – Kevan Furbank 978-1-78952-082-8
Hawkwind – Duncan Harris 978-1-78952-052-1
Roy Harper – Opher Goodwin 978-1-78952-130-6
Iron Maiden – Steve Pilkington 978-1-78952-061-3
Jethro Tull – Jordan Blum 978-1-78952-016-3
Elton John in the 1970s – Peter Kearns 978-1-78952-034-7
Gong – Kevan Furbank 978-1-78952-082-8
The Incredible String Band – Tim Moon 978-1-78952-107-8
Iron Maiden – Steve Pilkington 978-1-78952-061-3
Judas Priest – John Tucker 978-1-78952-018-7
Kansas – Kevin Cummings 978-1-78952-057-6
Level 42 – Matt Philips 978-1-78952-102-3
Aimee Mann – Jez Rowden 978-1-78952-036-1
Joni Mitchell – Peter Kearns 978-1-78952-081-1
The Moody Blues – Geoffrey Feakes 978-1-78952-042-2
Mike Oldfield – Ryan Yard 978-1-78952-060-6
Tom Petty – Richard James 978-1-78952-128-3
Queen – Andrew Wild 978-1-78952-003-3
Renaissance – David Detmer 978-1-78952-062-0
The Rolling Stones 1963-80 – Steve Pilkington 978-1-78952-017-0
Steely Dan – Jez Rowden 978-1-78952-043-9
Steve Hackett – Geoffrey Feakes 978-1-78952-098-9
Thin Lizzy – Graeme Stroud 978-1-78952-064-4
Toto – Jacob Holm-Lupo 978-1-78952-019-4

U2 – Eoghan Lyng 978-1-78952-078-1
UFO – Richard James 978-1-78952-073-6
The Who – Geoffrey Feakes 978-1-78952-076-7
Roy Wood and the Move – James R Turner 978-1-78952-008-8
Van Der Graaf Generator – Dan Coffey 978-1-78952-031-6
Yes – Stephen Lambe 978-1-78952-001-9
Frank Zappa 1966 to 1979 – Eric Benac 978-1-78952-033-0
10CC – Peter Kearns 978-1-78952-054-5

Decades Series
Alice Cooper in the 1970s – Chris Sutton 978-1-78952-104-7
Curved Air in the 1970s – Laura Shenton 978-1-78952-069-9
Fleetwood Mac in the 1970s – Andrew Wild 978-1-78952-105-4
Focus in the 1970s – Stephen Lambe 978-1-78952-079-8
Marillion in the 1980s – Nathaniel Webb 978-1-78952-065-1
Pink Floyd In The 1970s – Georg Purvis 978-1-78952-072-9
The Sweet in the 1970s – Darren Johnson 978-1-78952-139-9
Uriah Heep in the 1970s – Steve Pilkington 978-1-78952-103-0

On Screen series
Carry On... – Stephen Lambe 978-1-78952-004-0
David Cronenberg – Patrick Chapman 978-1-78952-071-2
Doctor Who: The David Tennant Years – Jamie Hailstone 978-1-78952-066-8
Monty Python – Steve Pilkington 978-1-78952-047-7
Seinfeld Seasons 1 to 5 – Stephen Lambe 978-1-78952-012-5

Other Books
Babysitting A Band On The Rocks – G.D. Praetorius 978-1-78952-106-1
Derek Taylor: For Your Radioactive Children – Andrew Darlington 978-1-78952-038-5
Iggy and The Stooges On Stage 1967-1974 – Per Nilsen 978-1-78952-101-6
Jon Anderson and the Warriors – the road to Yes – David Watkinson 978-1-78952-059-0
Nu Metal: A Definitive Guide – Matt Karpe 978-1-78952-063-7
Tommy Bolin: In and Out of Deep Purple – Laura Shenton 978-1-78952-070-5
Maximum Darkness – Deke Leonard 978-1-78952-048-4
Maybe I Should've Stayed In Bed – Deke Leonard 978-1-78952-053-8
The Twang Dynasty – Deke Leonard 978-1-78952-049-1

and many more to come!

Would you like to write for Sonicbond Publishing?

We are mainly a music publisher, but we also occasionally publish in other genres including film and television. At Sonicbond Publishing we are always on the look-out for authors, particularly for our two main series, On Track and Decades.

Mixing fact with in depth analysis, the On Track series examines the entire recorded work of a particular musical artist or group. All genres are considered from easy listening and jazz to 60s soul to 90s pop, via rock and metal.

The Decades series singles out a particular decade in an artist or group's history and focuses on that decade in more detail than may be allowed in the On Track series.

While professional writing experience would, of course, be an advantage, the most important qualification is to have real enthusiasm and knowledge of your subject. First-time authors are welcomed, but the ability to write well in English is essential.

Sonicbond Publishing has distribution throughout Europe and North America, and all our books are also published in E-book form. Authors will be paid a royalty based on sales of their book. Further details about our books are available from www.sonicbondpublishing.com. To contact us, complete the contact form there or email info@sonicbondpublishing.co.uk